WE'LL EAT AGAIN

★

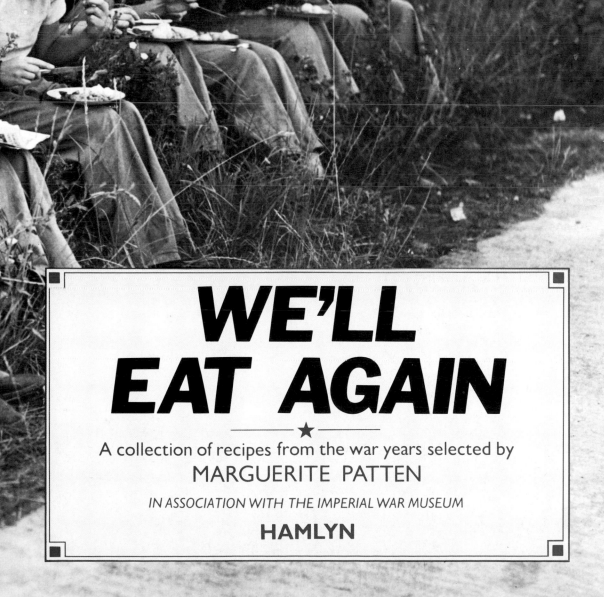

WE'LL
EAT AGAIN

★

A collection of recipes from the war years selected by
MARGUERITE PATTEN

IN ASSOCIATION WITH THE IMPERIAL WAR MUSEUM

HAMLYN

Marguerite Patten and the publishers would like to thank
Angela Holdsworth and the BBC for their help in providing some of
the recipes in the chapter 'After the War' which they found while
researching the major BBC television series *After The War Was Over*

Acknowledgements

Cover and inside photographs Hulton Picture Library
Patsy Cookstrips Mirror Group Newspapers
Recipes on pages 62, 85, 86 and 87 Cadbury Typhoo Ltd

First published in Great Britain in 1985
This edition published in 1990 by Hamlyn
an imprint of Reed Consumer Books Limited
Michelin House, 81 Fulham Road, London SW3 6RB
and Auckland, Melbourne, Singapore and Toronto

Reprinted 1990, 1991 (twice), 1992, 1993

A catalogue record for this book is available from the British Library

ISBN 0 600 32524 5

Produced by Mandarin Offset

Printed and bound in Hong Kong

Contents

Foreword

Rationing and austerity hardly seem promising subjects for a book and the bleak days of food shortages during the Second World War might appear to be of little relevance to us today. Yet a lot of people look back on those days with considerable nostalgia, remembering how they coped with the meagre rations of meat, eggs, and butter and the total absence of many foods that we now take for granted.

This book is an exercise in nostalgia, but it is arguably more than that. The health of the nation was surprisingly good during the war years, despite the physical and emotional stresses so many had to endure. Infant mortality declined and the average age of death from natural causes increased. Part of the reason for this may have been the new eating patterns which were forced on the British public by the war. For many of the poorer sections of the community rationing introduced more protein and vitamins, while for others it involved a reduction in the consumption of meat, fats, eggs, and sugar. The diet imposed by necessity was very much in line with the message of many doctors and nutritionists today, who campaign against high cholesterol and for high fibre in our food. The link between food and health is now generally recognised, so perhaps it is a good time to look again at the wartime recommendations of Lord Woolton, Potato Pete and Dr Carrot. Some of their tips and suggestions are now taken for granted, while others appear amusing or even lunatic. But the overriding intention, stressed by the Ministry of Food's newspaper advertisements and Kitchen Front radio broadcasts, was to make the best of what was available and to provide a simple healthy diet.

This book of recipes, illustrations, and cartoons taken from the Imperial War Museum's collections of Ministry of Food material, recalls how the housewives of Britain helped the war effort and kept the nation 'fighting fit'.

DR. ALAN BORG
Director, Imperial War Museum

Introduction

'You want to get through your work and difficulties with the same spirits you expect of the Forces in action . . . . Well, thanks to government planning, the foods that will feed you and your family to the pitch of fighting fitness are right at your hand. They have been deliberately chosen to that purpose. To release ships and seamen on the fighting fronts, you, on the 'Kitchen Front', have the job of using these foods to the greatest advantage. Here is how to do it: FIRST: *Your rations and allowances.* These are the *foundation* of your fighting diet. Take your full share of them always.

NEXT: *Vegetables.* These provide many of the vitamins so essential for good health and buoyant vitality.

THIRD: *Unrefined or whole-grain foods* – flour, oats, etc. These also supply valuable health factors, and, of course, add bulk to build up satisfying meals.

Spread your rations and allowances so that you get part of each of them *every* day, making sure that each member of your family gets his proper share.'

The words quoted above were from early material published by the Ministry of Food. These summarize the way we approached feeding our families during the war years and indeed for some time after the war ended.

When war was declared I was a Home Economist in the electrical industry and was used to giving cookery demonstrations that were based on delicious and lavish recipes; obviously these demonstrations were no longer possible. Instead we turned our attention to giving suggestions on the best ways to keep the family well fed. I co-operated with the local authority in Lincoln and in the evenings travelled around the villages to demonstrate to local groups. The Ministry of Food started publishing Food Facts in 1940 and I used their hints together with some of my own economical recipes.

I well remember visiting one local hall. The only appliance available was an elderly oil cooker. The caretaker cleaned this and the demonstration started. The cooker produced fumes and smoke like a London peasouper fog and the audience and I spent the session gasping for breath with tears raining down our cheeks. Fortunately in other places the equipment was rather more efficient.

In 1942 I went to the Ministry of Food as one of their Home Economists; I was based at Cambridge. My very first demonstration there took place in the market square. My colleagues and I erected our stall and demonstrated to the shoppers in the open market. We were in competition with the stallholders selling fruit, vegetables and other commodities, so we speedily learned to 'shout up'.

The Food Advice Division of the Ministry of Food gave demonstrations in our own centres, in markets and in the canteens of factories. We visited the outpatients departments in hospitals and welfare clinics to talk to patients, mothers-to-be and mothers of babies. We set up counters in large shops and demonstrated there with the help of small portable cookers. Many Home Economists drove small mobile vans and touring caravans, which were parked in convenient spots and the demonstration began as soon as passers-by gathered round. Our campaign was to find people, wherever they might be, and make them aware of the importance of keeping their families well fed on the rations available. Looking back I feel we were horribly bracing and we never sympathised with people over food problems if they grumbled. Most people, though, never complained and appreciated that we were trying to be helpful.

Perhaps this is a good place to recall the rations. These varied slightly from month to month as foods became slightly more or less plentiful. I have inserted metric measures – unknown in Britain at that time – so that younger people reading this book can appreciate the small amounts.

This is the ration for an adult *per week*:

Bacon and ham	4 oz (100 g)
Meat	to the value of 1s. 2d. (6p today). Sausages were not rationed but difficult to obtain; offal was originally unrationed but sometimes formed part of the meat ration.
Butter	2 oz (50 g)
Cheese	2 oz (50 g) sometimes it rose to 4 oz (100 g) and even up to 8 oz (225 g)
Margarine	4 oz (100 g)
Cooking fat	4 oz (100 g) often dropping to 2 oz (50 g)
Milk	3 pints (1800 ml) sometimes dropping to 2 pints (1200 ml). Household (skimmed, dried) milk was available, I think this was 1 packet each 4 weeks.
Sugar	8 oz (225 g)
Preserves	1 lb (450 g) every 2 months
Tea	2 oz (50 g)
Eggs	1 shell egg a week if available but at times dropping to 1 every two weeks. Dried eggs—1 packet each 4 weeks.
Sweets	12 oz (350 g) each 4 weeks.

In addition, there was a monthly points system. As an example of how these could be spent, the 16 points allowed you to buy one can of fish or meat or 2 lb (900 g) of dried fruit or 8 lb (3.6 kg) of split peas.

Babies and younger children, expectant and nursing mothers, had concentrated orange juice and cod liver oil from Welfare Clinics together with priority milk. This milk was also available to invalids.

During 1942 I was loaned to the scientific division of the Ministry of Food to go to various school canteens to assess the food value and vitamin content of school dinners. School meals were started during the war years to make quite certain that school children had the best possible main meal (remember most mothers were working long hours for the war effort).

The area in which I worked covered all East Anglia, and I was responsible for a second Food Advice Centre in Ipswich. As much of this was a rural area where large amounts of fruit were grown, I had a number of sessions in charge of 'Fruit Preservation Centres' in schools or other large kitchens where groups of ladies would gather to make preserves from local grown fruit and specially supplied sugar. The recipes were set by the Ministry of Food to ensure that the completed preserves could be stored and sold as part of the rations. The sessions were not entirely peaceful, for most ladies were experienced housewives, with their own very definite ideas on how jams should be made; some wanted to use their own recipes and addressed me firmly. 'Young woman, I was making jam before you were born'—quite right— but my job was to ensure that every completed pot of jam contained 60% sugar and was carefully sealed to ensure it really would keep well under all conditions, so I had to stand firm.

My work in East Anglia terminated when I left just before my daughter was born. I returned to the Ministry of Food—but this time in the London area—when she was several months old. I was fortunate enough to find a good nannie to care for the baby during the day. The work in London was similar to that in East Anglia but concentrated more on the big canteens, on factories, on hospitals and on public demonstrations.

At the end of 1943 I took over the Ministry of Food Advice Bureau at Harrods. This meant the end of travelling and the start of concentrated daily demonstrations.

I had two demonstrations each day from Monday to Friday and one on Saturday morning so that I was continually trying to find new ideas. The Ministry of Food leaflets were an invaluable guidance and many of the members of my audience a wonderful inspiration. Some people came from abroad and generously contributed ideas based on their own countries cuisine. A percentage of the people had never cooked before—they had relied on professional cooks. Imagine learning to cook at that particular time; in fact these people generally became inventive and clever cooks.

I was one of the contributors to the Kitchen Front early morning broadcasts on the B.B.C. and was able to pass on my favourite recipes to a wider audience.

Many of the ingredients available, such as dried egg and wartime (National) flour, were a challenge to any cook, but it was surprising how we learned to cope with these and produce edible dishes. As you follow the recipes you will find frequent mention of cups

(use a $\frac{1}{2}$ pint (300 ml) measure or breakfast cup). The teacup given in some recipes means a generous $\frac{1}{4}$ pint (150 ml) measure. The amounts of salt and pepper given are rather generous by todays standards so add these more sparingly.

Virtually every cook in Britain behaved like a zealous squirrel—we bottled and/or dried fresh fruits; we salted beans; we prepared economical chutneys and pickles; we made the very best use of every available ingredient. The chapter that begins on page 92 gives some of the most popular recipes.

As you read through this book you will find a wide variety of dishes, many of which are very much in keeping with the advice given by nutritionalists nowadays. We ate lots of vegetables and home-produced fruits but little fat, sugar or meat. Our menus may have been monotonous, but both adults and children were incredibly healthy and we all felt that we were playing a vital role towards the ultimate victory when we could all happily look forward to eating much more varied and exciting dishes once again.

IMPORTANT FACTS

The phraseology used in the book is that given in the original recipes and may need a little explaining, for example we always talked about 'tinned' and not 'canned' foods.

Dried eggs

This refers to the dried egg powder available on rations books. This was pure egg with all the moisture removed. To reconstitute dried egg blend 1 LEVEL tablespoon dried egg powder with 2 tablespoons water (this is the equivalent of a fresh egg). If people were generous with the amount of dried egg powder they were inclined to have a somewhat unpleasant taste. In some recipes the egg powder could be used dry from the tin.

Measures

The term GILL is used in some recipes, this was very popular until after the second world war when it was no longer used as it seemed to cause confusion.

1 gill equals $\frac{1}{4}$ pint in recipes

A dessertspoon measure was frequently used, this is equivalent to a good $\frac{1}{2}$ tablespoon.

Household milk

This was the skimmed milk powder available on rations books. It was blended with water to make the equivalent of fresh milk. Put 1 pint of lukewarm water into a container. Measure 4 level tablespoons of the milk powder and sprinkle it—a little at a time—on top of the water while beating briskly with an egg whisk, fork or wooden spoon.

Oven temperatures

In some recipes the oven settings may appear high by today's standards. This is because most of the recipes contained relatively little fat and speedy baking could be recommended.

The equivalent descriptions and modern settings are given below. The term very moderate used to be given; nowadays many people do not use these words.

A very cool oven: often called very slow or very low is 90–120°C, 200–250°F, Gas Mark 0–$\frac{1}{2}$

A cool oven: often called slow or low is 140–150°C, 275–300°F, Gas Mark 1–2

A very moderate oven: nowadays generally called moderate is 160°C, 325°F, Gas Mark 3

A moderate oven: is 180°C, 350°F, Gas Mark 4

A moderately hot oven: is 190–200°C, 375–400°F, Gas Mark 5–6

A hot oven: is 220°C, 425°F, Gas Mark 7

A very hot oven: is 230–240°C, 450–475°F, Gas Mark 8–9

Soups

A flask of soup was very comforting on a cold winter night when firewatching or on Home Guard Duty, or even to take down to the shelter. The more substantial ones made nourishing lunches or suppers. We learnt to make delicious stocks from vegetable trimmings and a few bacon rinds and to thicken soups with oatmeal or to pack them with root vegetables or beans for a filling meal.

When you come home tired and cold after a long day's work, there's nothing so cheering for you as soup. Thick soup is nourishing, a meal in itself. Soup is very easy to digest, an important point when you are tired. And, if you keep a soup-pot handy on the stove, soup is as easy to make as A B C. Look after your soup-pot and then make one of these delicious soups for the evening.

War-work and Home-work

BORTSCH

Cooking time: 2 hours 5 minutes   *Quantity:* 4 helpings

1 oz dripping or margarine
1 large raw beetroot, peeled and grated
2 potatoes, peeled and chopped or grated
1 carrot, peeled and chopped or grated
1 onion, peeled and chopped and grated

12 oz cabbage, chopped or grated
2 tomatoes, chopped
2 bay leaves
water or stock (see method)
salt and pepper
pinch mixed herbs
chopped parsley

METHOD: Melt the dripping or margarine in a pan and fry the beetroot for about 5 minutes. Put all the vegetables and bay leaves into a saucepan, together with the beetroot. Completely cover with water or stock and bring to the boil. Remove any scum, put on the lid and simmer slowly for 2 hours. Add seasoning and pinch of mixed herbs. Serve garnished with parsley.

I used to think one didn't oughter
Make a soup from vegetable water.
But this, my dear – this IS a snorter!

Forward the Soup Pot

If you can use stock for the basis of your soups they will be all the better for it, more nourishing, more tasty. The *soup-pot* need not use up hours of fuel. Put your root vegetables (all except turnips), bacon rinds, etc., in a large pot with plenty of water. Cook slowly for $\frac{1}{2}$ hour. Boil vigorously for a minute or two then put straight into the hay box or into the oven when the baking is done to use up the last of the heat. The soup-pot should be brought to the boil every day. Green vegetables and outside leaves may be added to the stock if it is to be used at once. Don't disturb the fat on top of the stock for this preserves the flavour, but remove before use. When you want to make a soup you just take some of this stock, add what flavourings or vegetables you fancy as in the recipes on these pages and in a very short time your soup will be ready.

VEGETABLE SOUP

METHOD: Fry 2 oz rolled oats or oatmeal in 1 oz margarine. Blend with a little of 2 pints of water, then add the rest of the water and bring to boil. Add 3 potatoes, 4 carrots, $\frac{1}{2}$ small swede, 1 leek if you have it, sliced or cut into cubes. Cook for 1 hour. Just before serving add pepper and salt and some chopped parsley. The quantities given are sufficient for 4 helpings.

QUICK VEGETABLE SOUP

Cooking time: 30 minutes   *Quantity:* 4 helpings

½ oz dripping
12 oz mixed vegetables, diced
1½ pints water or stock

salt and pepper
chopped parsley

METHOD: Melt the dripping in a saucepan, add the vegetables and cook gently in the fat for a good 5 minutes. Add the liquid and simmer slowly for 25 minutes. Season the soup, then rub through a sieve to make a purée. Reheat and serve sprinkled with chopped parsley.

QUICK SOUP

Cooking time: 30 minutes   *Quantity:* 6 helpings

4 breakfast cups stock or
  water
1 lb mixed vegetables
1–1½ teaspoons salt
2 tablespoons wheatmeal
  flour

1 tablespoon household milk
chopped parsley or
  watercress or sliced
  cabbage

METHOD: Put 3 breakfastcups of stock or water on to boil, then wash and grate or shred the vegetables. Add salt and vegetables to stock and cook till tender, season. Blend flour and household milk with 1 breakfast cup of water and pour on to the soup, stir and cook for 3–5 minutes. Serve with parsley, watercress or cabbage.

THE LITTLE EXTRA THAT MAKES ALL THE DIFFERENCE!

Try serving some of these favourites with your soup.

Dumplings
Mix 8 oz flour with 1 teaspoon baking powder and 1 teaspoonful sweet herbs. Form into a firm dough with cold water. Drop into soup and cook quickly for 7–10 minutes before serving.

Croûtons
Take a few slices of wheatmeal bread, dice and bake on a tin till crisp and brown.

Wheatmeal Rusks
Cut stale wheatmeal bread in ½ in thick fingers and bake in a cool oven till crisp. You can utilise the heat which remains in your oven after you have been cooking for this purpose.

QUESTIONS YOU ASK

Can you give me a new soup recipe?
    Here's a delicious one: *Golden Barley Soup.* Grate or mince 2 lb. of carrots, put with 1 small teacup of barley into 1 quart of water and simmer for 2½ hours. Roll a piece of margarine the size of a walnut in 1 tablespoonful of flour and stir it into the soup. Cook fast for 8 minutes, season. Serves 4 or 5 helpings.

CREAM OF PARSNIP SOUP

Cooking time: 25–30 minutes   *Quantity:* 6 helpings

3 pints stock or water
1–1½ lb parsnips
½ leek
3 teaspoons salt
pepper

2 oz flour
¼ pint household milk
2 tablespoons chopped
  parsley

METHOD: Put stock or water on to boil while shredding the parsnips and leek. When boiling add shredded parsnips and leek. Boil for 20 minutes, season, add blended flour and milk and simmer for 3–5 minutes, stirring all the time. Serve with parsley.

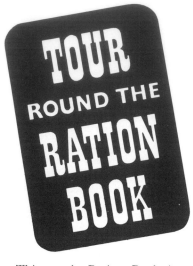

This year's Ration Book is a much simpler affair than last year's three books, and you should get familiar with it from the start. So here we take you on a conducted tour, with stops at the principal objects of interest! Cut this out and read it with the Ration Book in front of you. Then you will see how simple it has all been made.

THE CHILD'S BOOK
R.B.2. will be used in exactly the same way except that the tea coupons will be marked when oranges are bought, and will not be cut out.

YOUR OLD RATION BOOKS should be kept until the end of August. They may still be needed – for instance for July preserves, or your first tin of dried eggs. If they contain special authorisations keep them until these are used up. Do not transfer them to your new book.

THE FRONT COVER. Check the entries with your identity card. If there is any difference report it to the Food Office.

PAGE 2 You should by now have filled in the details at X. See that they agree with those on the front cover. Fill in Y if under 18. Leave Z alone.

PAGE 5 is the first of the coupon pages. See how they are now all divided (Points as well) into four-weekly periods numbered 1 to 13. This will help you to "keep your place" and make shopping easier. You have re-registered by now of course, so the counterfoils have been cut out by the shops. You need not fill in the spaces marked B unless you deposit whole pages with your retailer.

PAGE 9 now combines in one the coupons for butter, margarine and cooking fats.

PAGE 11 will be used for the ordinary and the special ration of cheese.

PAGE 13 will record your purchase of eggs. Remember that you won't get them every week. Poultry keepers will get no shell eggs.

PAGE 15 combines sugar and preserves. The squares marked Q, R, S will not be used at present.

PAGE 17 Tea coupons will be cut out by the retailer, four at a time.

PAGES 25 TO 34 are Points Coupon pages. They are just the same as those in the old pink book but the four-week periods are referred to by number instead of date.

PAGE 25 MUST CONTAIN THE NAMES AND ADDRESSES OF YOUR RETAILERS. It is illegal to use the Ration Book if these are not filled in. The column on the left is for noting the deposit of whole pages.

PAGE 39 Fill in if you deposit any rows of Points Coupons, also fill in the bottom line if you deposit your tea coupon page. Note this specially because it is new.

BACK COVER (page 40) has two panels. Panel 1 (at the top) will be used for soap, which may still be bought at any time during the four-weekly period. Panel 2 will not be used yet.

OATMEAL SOUP

Cooking time: 1 hour   *Quantity:* 4 helpings

"I'll put pep in your step." *says Potato Pete*

1 oz margarine
2 medium onions, grated or finely diced
2 tablespoons medium oatmeal
1 pint cold water
salt and pepper
½ pint milk
3 medium carrots, grated

METHOD: Heat the margarine in a pan, add the onions and cook for 5 minutes. Blend the oatmeal with the cold water, tip into the pan and stir as the mixture comes to the boil; season lightly. Simmer steadily for 30 minutes, stirring frequently, then add the milk and carrots and cook for a further 15 minutes.

CHEESE SOUP

Cooking time: 25 minutes   *Quantity:* 4 helpings

2 tablespoons chopped onion or leek, if possible
1½ oz margarine
2 cups household milk
2 cups water
2 tablespoons flour
1 cup grated cheese
salt and pepper
2 tablespoons chopped parsley

METHOD: Add onion and margarine to milk and water, bring to the boil, cook for 15 minutes, stirring all the time. (Remember household milk catches more easily than ordinary milk, so stirring is important.) Blend flour with a little milk, stir in and cook for a few minutes to thicken. Add cheese and seasoning. Stir until the cheese is melted, but do not boil again. Add parsley and serve very hot.

POTATO AND WATERCRESS SOUP

Cooking time: 40 minutes   *Quantity:* 4 helpings

1 lb potatoes
1 pint vegetable stock
1 teaspoon margarine
1 pint household milk
pepper and salt
2 bunches watercress

MF FOOD IS A MUNITION OF WAR — DON'T WASTE IT

METHOD: Wash and peel potatoes and chop in small pieces. Cook potatoes in stock till soft, mash against side of pan with wooden spoon, add margarine, milk and seasoning. Reheat and just before serving add chopped watercress.

MINESTRONE SOUP

Cooking time: 2 hours **Ingredients:** 3 oz haricot beans, 1½ pints water, 2 oz quick cooking macaroni, salt and pepper, 1 oz dripping or oil, 1 onion, peeled and finely grated, 1 stick celery, chopped, ½ tablespoon chopped parsley, 8 oz tomatoes, fresh or bottled or tinned, chopped, 8 oz cabbage, chopped, 1 pint water, grated cheese. **Quantity:** 4 helpings

Soak the beans for 24 hours in the 1½ pints of water. Cook slowly for 1½ hours or until soft then strain. Cook the macaroni for 7 minutes in a saucepan of boiling salted water then strain. Heat the dripping or oil, fry the onion, celery and parsley for 5 minutes. Add the tomatoes, cabbage and 1 pint water and bring to the boil. Put in the beans, macaroni and seasoning to taste. Simmer for 20 minutes. Serve sprinkled with grated cheese. This soup is very thick but a little extra liquid could be used for a thinner soup.

MOCK OYSTER SOUP

Cooking time: 1 hour 10 minutes   *Quantity:* 4 helpings

1–1½ lb fish trimmings	1 small onion or leek, sliced
1 teaspoon salt	8 oz artichokes, peeled and
1 pint water, plus extra water	sliced
1 blade mace	½ teaspoon pepper
6 white peppercorns	2 tablespoons flour
1 clove	¼ pint milk
2 teaspoons mixed herbs	chopped parsley

METHOD: Wash the fish and cook in the salted water with the mace, peppercorns, clove and mixed herbs in a muslin bag, and onion or leek for 30 minutes. Strain off the stock and make up to 1 pint with water. Cook the artichokes in the stock for 30 minutes. Add the pepper and sieve. Blend the flour with the milk, add to the soup and stir until it boils. Cook gently for a further 5 minutes. Sprinkle with chopped parsley before serving.

★   ★   ★

HOLLANDAISE SOUP

Cooking time: 10 minutes   *Quantity:* 4 helpings

1 oz margarine	salt and pepper
1 oz flour	3 tablespoons cream from top
¾ pint white stock or water	of milk or unsweetened
with few drops flavouring,	evaporated milk
e.g. beef extract	1 tablespoon peas
¼ pint milk	1 tablespoon diced cucumber
1 reconstituted dried egg or 1	or gherkin
shell egg	

METHOD: Melt the margarine in a pan, stir in the flour. Cook for 3 minutes, remove the pan from the heat and gradually stir in the stock, or water and flavouring, and milk. Bring to the boil and cook until thickened. Add the egg and seasoning to taste. Cook *very slowly* for a further 3 minutes. Add the cream or milk. Garnish with peas and diced cucumber or gherkin.

FISH SOUP

Cooking time: 20 minutes.   *Quantity:* 4 helpings

1 oz margarine	salt and pepper
2 oz flour	1 tablespoon chopped parsley
2 pints fish stock (see under method)	1 reconstituted dried egg or 1 fresh egg
¼ pint milk	watercress

A CHRISTMAS GIFT

Everyone, grown-up or child, who has to take packed lunches, craves for a good *hot* lunch now and then, and therefore would welcome the gift of a portable hay-box. Soup, stew, sausage and mash, shepherd's pie, or any other favourite dish keeps *really* hot in this box, for several hours. You can make the portable hay-box from a spare gas-mask carrier. It's very simple. Full directions will be sent if you write to the Ministry of Food.

METHOD: Melt the margarine in a pan, stir in the flour and cook for several minutes, stirring well. Remove from the heat and gradually add the fish stock. Boil steadily until the soup thickens, then add the milk, seasoning and parsley. Whisk in the egg. Stir over a gentle heat, do not allow the soup to boil, for a further 5 minutes. Serve garnished with watercress.

To Make Fish Stock

Fish trimmings are invaluable to make an interesting stock. The fish bones, fish heads and skins should be used.

Put the fish trimmings into a pan with water to cover, add a peeled onion, a little chopped celery, a pinch of mixed herbs and seasoning. Cook slowly for 30 minutes, no longer. Strain.

SCOTCH BROTH

Cooking time: 2½–3 hours   *Quantity:* 4 helpings

1 oz pearl barley	1 lb swede, peeled and diced
8 oz stewing beef, diced	salt and pepper
2 pints water	2 oz cabbage, sliced
3 oz onions or leeks, sliced	1 tablespoon chopped parsley
8 oz carrots, diced	

METHOD: Put the barley into cold water, bring to the boil then strain.

Put the barley, beef and 2 pints water in a pan; bring to the boil and skim. Simmer for 1 hour then add the prepared onions or leeks, carrots and swede with the seasoning. Cook for 1½ to 2 hours. Add the cabbage 15 minutes before serving. Skim any surplus fat off the soup. Remove the meat with a perforated spoon. Place the chopped parsley in a soup tureen, pour in the broth. The meat is served as a separate course.

Pea Pod Soup

Wash the pods thoroughly and place in a deep saucepan. Add 2 sprigs of mint, 1 large potato, and chives, onion or spring onion (if available), a good pinch of salt and pepper, and cover with boiling water. Cook with the lid on until tender. Rub the vegetables and the pods through sieve, then return to the saucepan. Blend a little flour (1 oz to each pint) with cold water, add some of the hot soup to it. Return all to the saucepan and stir until boiling and the soup is creamy. Serve very hot.

Main Meals

With less meat than in peace-time and heavier demands on our milk supplies, we looked around for other body-building foods to help out. Two new ones were available in plenty; fresh-salted cod from Iceland and white haricot beans from across the Atlantic. These formed the basis of many delicious recipes and certainly helped to give us a nutritionally balanced diet.

TO THE FISHMONGER

Your customers will like the Fresh-Salted Cod but a lot depends on the care taken in de-salting. Soak in cold water, with the skin uppermost for 24 to 48 hours; if there is much fish in relation to water, change the water—probably more than once. Always add bicarbonate of soda to the water; one heaped teaspoon to 1 gallon. Never de-salt more than required for the day's sales and explain to your customers that Fresh-Salted Cod must be treated as fresh fish and cooked the day it is bought.

FOOD FACTS

More good news on the Kitchen Front—extra fish is now coming into the country; regular supplies of a new type of fish—Fresh-Salted Cod. It's almost free from bones, it's easy to cook, and there's no waste. Above all—it's cheap: the maximum retail price is 9d. per lb.

Fresh-Salted Cod requires soaking in water for 48 hours before cooking. Your fishmonger will do this and when you buy it, it will be ready to cook.

BAKED FISH CAKES

Cooking time: 20 minutes   *Quantity:* 4 helpings

4 oz cooked fresh-salted cod
1 lb mashed potatoes
2 large well-mashed carrots
1 teaspoon mixed sweet
  herbs

1 dessertspoon Worcester
  sauce
1 rasher of bacon cooked and
  chopped, if liked
browned breadcrumbs

METHOD: Mix ingredients thoroughly, form into small round cakes and roll each in fine, well-baked breadcrumbs. Put the cakes on greased baking tin and bake for 20 minutes in a moderate oven. This is a particularly good way of making fish cakes as no fat is required.

FISH PIE (1)

Cooking time: 30 minutes   *Quantity:* 4 helpings

1 pint white or parsley sauce
¾ lb cooked fresh-salted cod
1 lb sliced cooked carrots or
  swedes

1 lb sliced cooked potatoes
chopped parsley
pepper
browned breadcrumbs

METHOD: Put a layer of sauce at the bottom of a dish, arrange in alternate layers the fish and vegetables and sauce, finishing with potatoes. Sprinkle the parsley and seasoning between the layers. Cover the top with crisped breadcrumbs (much improved if tossed in bacon fat). Put the dish into a moderate oven to get thoroughly hot.

FISH PIE (2)

Follow the directions for the Fish Pie on this page but add 2 sliced cooking apples to the other ingredients.

STEAMED FISH ROLL

Cooking time: 1½ hours   *Quantity:* 4 helpings

PASTRY
8 oz self-raising flour or plain
    flour with 1 teaspoon
    baking powder
2 oz suet, chopped
2 oz raw potato, grated
water to bind
FILLING
4 oz fresh-salted cod, cut into
    small pieces

6 oz vegetables (cauliflower,
    grated raw or cooked
    mashed carrots or parsnips
    or swedes or cooked peas)
1 tablespoon brown gravy or
    sauce
1 teaspoon vinegar
pepper

METHOD: Make a dough with the flour, or flour and baking powder, suet and raw potato and enough water to make a stiff dough. Roll out, spread with the fish and vegetables moistened with gravy or sauce and the vinegar. Dust with pepper, roll up. Wrap the roll in greased paper and steam for 1½ hours. Serve with gravy or sauce.

SUET CRUST PASTRY

You save suet by using grated potato, as in the recipe above for Steamed Fish Roll.

Our Sailors don't mind risking their lives to feed you—and your family—but they do mind if you help the U-boats by wasting food.

CURRIED COD

Cooking time: 10 minutes   *Quantity:* for 4 people

1 tablespoon dripping
1 tomato or 2 or 3 spring
    onions if possible
1 tablespoon gravy powder
1 dessertspoon curry powder
about 1 pint vegetable
    boilings or water

1 tablespoon chutney or
    stewed apple
1 dessertspoon sugar
OTHER INGREDIENTS
1 lb fresh-salted cod, either
    boiled or baked
1 lb sliced cooked carrots

METHOD: Melt the dripping, fry the tomato or onions cut small, stir in the gravy powder and curry powder. When it is well bound, gradually add boiling liquid to form a thick sauce. Stir in the chutney or apple and sugar. Add the fish and the carrots cut in small pieces and simmer for 5 to 10 minutes. Serve with plenty of plain boiled potatoes.

FISH ENVELOPE

Cooking time: 20–30 minutes   *Quantity:* 4 helpings

MASHED POTATO PASTRY
8 tablespoons national flour
4 tablespoons mashed potato
2 oz fat
FILLING
12 tablespoons cooked mixed
  vegetables, mashed

salt and pepper
4 oz cooked or tinned fish,
  well drained
$\frac{1}{2}$ teacup thick white sauce

METHOD: Blend the flour and potato together, soften the fat slightly and blend in with the potato mixture. It is rarely necessary to add any water to bind. Roll out thinly and divide in two. Spread one piece with the cooked vegetables mashed and seasoned. Cream the fish with the white sauce and spread on the other piece of pastry. Put together and bake in a hot oven for 20–30 minutes. Eat hot or cold.

Night and day men of the Royal Navy cheerfully risk their lives to guard your food. They don't mind danger but waste gives them the creeps!

FISH IN SAVOURY CUSTARD

Cooking time: 45 minutes   *Quantity:* 4 helpings

4 small fillets of fish or 2 fish
  cutlets
1 egg or 1 reconstituted egg
$\frac{1}{2}$ pint milk

salt and pepper
1 teaspoon chopped parsley
small pinch mixed herbs

METHOD: Arrange the fillets or cutlets in a greased dish. If possible, roll these. Beat the egg, pour on the milk. If using dried egg, the milk should be poured on boiling. Add seasoning, parsley and herbs. Pour over the fish and bake in a very moderate oven for approximately 45 minutes. It is advisable, as with all baked custards, to stand the dish in another containing cold water.

COD CASSEROLE

METHOD: Skin $1\frac{1}{2}$ lb fresh-salted cod, bring to boil, simmer 15 to 20 minutes, flake and remove any bones. Parboil and slice thinly 1 lb parsnips. Slice one small cabbage crossways. Arrange in layers in a pie dish or stewing jar, sprinkling each layer with a little chopped parsley, leek when possible, and small pieces of margarine. Blend a dessertspoon of cornflour with 1 pint of water, pour in. Cover with lid or paper, bake in moderate oven 40 minutes.

FISH CHARLOTTE

Cooking time: ¾ to 1 hour   *Quantity:* 4 helpings

8 oz bread (equals 6 slices)
a little fish paste
¾ lb fish
4 tablespoons chopped
    parsley

1½ teaspoons lemon substitute
salt and pepper

METHOD: Spread the slices of bread on both sides with the paste. Cut one of the slices to fit the bottom of the basin. Remove crusts. Line the rest of the basin with slices of bread, cut in strips. Chop up the crusts into small dice. Cover the fish with boiling water and leave for 1 to 2 minutes. Take out, remove the skin and bones and flake into smallish pieces. Add parsley, lemon substitute, and salt and pepper to taste. Put a layer of fish into the basin, cover with the diced crusts and pack in alternative layers, until the basin is filled, finishing with a layer of diced crusts. Press down well, cover with an upturned saucer and steam for ¾ to 1 hour. Serve hot with a green vegetable or cold with a salad.

BAKED FISH WITH MASHED TURNIPS

Cooking time: 45 minutes   *Quantity:* 4 or 5 helpings

1 large fillet fresh-salted cod
pepper
2 oz margarine
2 lb turnips, peeled and diced
salt

2 tablespoons flour
1 pint turnip water and milk
3 tablespoons capers or
    mustard

METHOD: Put the fish in a baking tin or fireproof dish, season well with pepper and put the margarine, cut in small pieces on top. Cover with a paper and bake for 30 minutes in a slow oven.

Cook the turnips in salted water until tender. Drain thoroughly and mash with pepper. Keep very hot.

Make the sauce by pouring off as much fat as possible from the fish into a saucepan. Stir in the flour and blend well over a very low heat. Gradually stir in the pint of turnip water and milk, cook until smooth and creamy. Add the capers or mustard to taste.

Make a bed of the mashed turnips, dish the fish on it and pour over the sauce.

RECIPE of the WEEK

FISH HOT POT

Cooking time: ¾ hour
Ingredients: 1 lb white fish, filleted, little flour, salt and pepper, 4 oz grated cheese, 1½ lb sliced potatoes, vegetable stock or household milk or water, chopped parsley. **Quantity:** 4 helpings

Cut the fillets of fish into pieces. Roll in flour and put in a greased fire-proof dish. Sprinkle with salt and pepper, then with grated cheese, and cover with a layer of potatoes. Pour in vegetable stock, household milk or water to fill a quarter of the dish. Cook in moderate oven for three quarters of an hour. Sprinkle with plenty of chopped parsley.

Experiment with your meals as much as you can. It gives variety and it does you good.

BROWN FISH STEW WITH BEANS

Cooking time: 25 minutes **Ingredients:** 1 oz dripping or cooking fat, 1 lb white fish, diced, 8 oz onions, sliced, 2 tomatoes, sliced, 1 tablespoon flour, 1–2 teaspoons gravy browning, ½ pint fish stock or water, 1 teaspoon Worcester sauce (optional), salt and pepper, 8 oz cooked or canned haricot beans. **Quantity:** 4 helpings

Heat the dripping or fat in a large saucepan. Add the fish and heat until golden brown then carefully remove from the pan. Put in the onions and tomatoes, cook for a few minutes, then stir in the flour and gravy browning. Blend in the fish stock or water and Worcester sauce, if using this, and a little seasoning. Bring to the boil, stir until slightly thickened, then return the fish to the pan. Heat for a few minutes, add the beans and continue heating for 3–4 minutes.

FISH BAKE

Cooking time: 30 minutes   *Quantity:* 4 helpings

1 lb potatoes, grated
salt and pepper
2 large onions, grated
2 tablespoons chopped
  parsley

1½ lb fish, cooked and
  flaked—cod, haddock,
  hake or mackerel
¼ pint milk

METHOD: Grease a shallow casserole well. Put a layer of grated potato on the bottom, season well, add a sprinkling of the onion and parsley, then a layer of fish; continue filling the casserole like this ending with potato. Pour over the milk. Cover with a piece of greased paper, then put on the lid. Bake in the centre of a moderately hot oven for a good 30 minutes. This may be served hot or cold.

USEFUL FUEL-SAVERS

Warm foods are not the only 'warming foods'—you don't need a hot meal every day.

Never heat the oven for one cake or pudding, plan a baking day.

Try to arrange with neighbours to share ovens. One day one neighbour could cook two or three joints; another day, someone's milk pudding might be tucked into a not quite full oven, or a cake baked while a casserole is slowly cooking. While you are doing this, you are not just helping each other. You are helping the Miners who work to provide our fuel.

DEVILLED HERRINGS

Cooking time: 15 minutes   *Quantity:* 4 helpings

4 medium sized herrings
½ oz margarine
1 teaspoon made mustard
1 teaspoon vinegar
1 teaspoon Worcester sauce

pinch salt
1 tablespoon sugar
¼ pint water
1 onion, grated
½ teaspoon pickling spice

METHOD: Split the herrings and take out the backbones. Cream the margarine, add the mustard, vinegar, Worcester sauce, salt and sugar. Spread this paste on the herrings. Roll tightly. Put into a saucepan with the water, onion and pickling spice. Simmer gently for a good 10 minutes. Serve hot or cold.

Mackerel may be cooked in the same way, but they will take slightly longer.

FISH FLAN

Cooking time: 35 minutes   *Quantity:* 4 helpings

pastry made with 6 oz flour, etc, see pages 52 and 53
2 tablespoons chopped onion
½ oz dripping
3 tablespoons flour
1 teaspoon paprika
½ pint milk and water
1 teaspoon salt
1 tablespoon vinegar
1 lb white fish, steamed and flaked
chopped parsley

METHOD: Line an 8 inch sandwich tin or flan ring with the pastry and bake blind in a moderately hot oven for 20 minutes. Fry the onion in the dripping for 5 minutes without browning, stir in the flour and paprika and cook for 1 minute. Add the liquid and bring to the boil, stirring all the time, and boil gently for 5 minutes. Add the salt, vinegar and fish; heat through and turn into the hot flan case. Garnish with chopped parsley.

★   ★   ★

HERRING PLATE PIE

Cooking time: 25–30 minutes   *Quantity:* 4 helpings

1½ oz cooking fat or margarine
6 oz plain flour
½ teaspoon salt
2 tablespoons finely grated raw potato
water to mix, if necessary
4 tablespoons grated raw potato
6 tablespoons chopped celery
8 tablespoons chopped leek
½ tablespoon vinegar
¼ teaspoon grated nutmeg
1 teaspoon salt
pinch of pepper
½ tin herrings (12 oz size)

METHOD: Rub the fat or margarine into the flour and salt. Add the finely grated potato and mix to a stiff dough with water. Roll out half the pastry and line an 8 inch ovenproof pie plate or tin. Place half the grated potato, celery and leek on the pastry and sprinkle with the vinegar, nutmeg and seasoning. Cut the herrings in half lengthways, place on the mixture and add the remainder of the potato, celery and leek. Roll out the remaining pastry and cover the pie. Make an inch slit on the top. Bake in a hot oven for 25–30 minutes.

PILCHARD LAYER LOAF

This is something new and very nice.
Cooking time: 30 minutes, plus time to make sauce **Ingredients:** 1 small national wheatmeal loaf, 1 5-oz tin pilchard (4 points), ¾ pint thick white sauce, see page 69, 1 teaspoon mustard, 2 tablespoons vinegar, salt and pepper. **Quantity:** 4 helpings

Cut off the crusts (using them later for toast or rusks) and slice the loaf lengthwise into four. Spread each slice with pilchards mashed with a little sauce and seasoning. If the pilchards are not packed in tomato sauce you may care to add a little piquant sauce to this mixture. Dip the layers in water to moisten, then place one on top of the other to re-form a loaf. All this can be done in advance. When required, place the pilchard loaf in a fireproof dish and pour over the sauce, mixed with the mustard, vinegar and seasoning. Bake in a moderate oven for about 30 minutes. Serve with green vegetable.

This is the question of the week: *Did you get your National Wholemeal Bread?* More and more bakers are baking it now, but if you can't get it locally write to the Ministry of Food, London, giving the name and address of your baker.

DINNER FOR A KING

Bakehouse Mutton makes a good, satisfying, heartening mid-day meal. Here is how to make it for 4 or 5 people.

Scrub 2½ lb potatoes and cut into thick slices. Put in a baking tin and season with salt and pepper. Pour over a teacup of water. Roll up 2 breasts of lamb (boned), lay them on top of the potatoes, cover with margarine papers and bake in a moderate oven for 1½ hours. Remove the paper and brown the meat for about 20 minutes before serving.

ARTICHOKES IN CHEESE BATTER

Cooking time: 30 minutes   *Quantity:* 4 helpings

1 lb artichokes
salt and pepper
4 oz plain flour
1 tablespoon dried egg

¼ pint milk or milk and water
2–3 oz cheese, grated
1 teaspoon baking powder
little fat for frying

METHOD: Scrub the artichokes and boil in salted water until tender. Peel and cut in thick slices. Mix the flour, seasoning and egg, add enough of the milk, or milk and water, to make a thick batter, beat well; add the remaining liquid. Lastly add the cheese and baking powder. Heat the fat in a frying pan, dip the artichoke slices in the batter and fry in the hot fat until golden brown.

Alternatively the artichokes may be mixed with the batter and baked in the oven in the same way as a Yorkshire pudding, see page 100.

BACON TURNOVERS (1)

Cooking time: 30 minutes   *Quantity:* 4 helpings

PASTRY
12 oz self-raising flour or
plain flour with 3
teaspoons baking powder
pinch salt
3 oz cooking fat or bacon fat,
see method
water

FILLING
4 oz fat bacon rashers
2 cooked leeks, finely
chopped
8 oz cooked potatoes, diced
1–2 tablespoons chopped
parsley

METHOD: Sift the flour and salt, rub in the cooking fat. You could use the fat that runs from the bacon if it is allowed to become cold, see page 37, instead of the cooking fat. Bind with water. Grill and chop the bacon rashers, cool then mix with the leeks, potatoes and parsley. Roll out the pastry and cut into 4 large rounds. Put the bacon mixture in the centre of each round; moisten the edges of the pastry with water. Fold over to make a turnover shape and seal firmly. Bake in the middle of a hot oven for 25 minutes until crisp and brown. Serve hot or cold.

There is another recipe on page 37.

BEAN MEDLEY

Cooking time: 1½ hours **Ingredients:** ¾ lb haricot beans (soaked overnight), 1½ pints water, salt and pepper, 1 tablespoon treacle, 1½ lb mixed vegetables (carrots, parsnips, leeks etc), diced, 2 oz grilled chopped bacon, chopped parsley. **Quantity:** 4 helpings

Soak the beans overnight and put them into a pan with water, pepper and treacle. Partly boil. Add salt and diced vegetables and cook until tender and the water absorbed. Dish up, cover with the bacon and sprinkle with chopped parsley. Serve with bread and butter and watercress.

SAVOURY CHARLOTTE

Cooking time: about 1 hour   *Quantity:* 4–5 helpings

2 lb mixed vegetables
salt and pepper
2 rashers streaky bacon
1 small wheatmeal loaf

1 tablespoon wheatmeal flour
3 tablespoons chopped
  parsley

METHOD: Prepare and slice the vegetables and cook until tender in just enough water to cover, seasoning with salt and pepper. Cut off the bacon rinds and cook with the vegetables. Grill the rashers. Cut slices of bread about $\frac{1}{4}$ in thick to fit the top and bottom of a cake tin (don't use the crusts). Then cut the rest of the bread into fingers about 1 in wide and $\frac{1}{2}$ in thick and the same height as your cake tin. Dip all the bread into the fat from the grilled bacon. Cover the bottom of the tin with the slice of bread and press the fingers neatly round the side, fitting them closely together.

When the vegetables are cooked, drain them (saving the liquid of course) and mash thoroughly with a fork. Make a $\frac{1}{2}$ pint of parsley sauce by thickening the vegetable liquid with the flour and adding 2 tablespoons of the parsley and add it to the mash. Stir in the bacon, chopped small, and pour the mixture into the cake tin. Fit the lid of bread on top. Cover with a margarine paper. Bake in a moderate oven for about 30 minutes when the charlotte should turn out firm and crisp. Sprinkle with parsley and serve with parsley sauce or brown gravy.

RECIPE of the WEEK

CANADIAN BAKE

Cooking time: 2 hours
Soak $1\frac{1}{2}$ lb small white haricots for 24 hours then simmer till quite soft (about $1\frac{1}{2}$ hours). Mash well and mix with 1 lb mashed potatoes and $\frac{1}{4}$ lb chopped boiled American bacon. Flavour with a dessertspoon of sage, teaspoon of sugar and some pepper. If too stiff, add a little bean water. Sprinkle sides and bottom of a greased pie-dish with breadcrumbs. Press the mixture well in, cover with a greased paper and bake in a moderate oven for about 30 minutes. Serve with cabbage and gravy. **Quantity:** 6 helpings

CHINESE CAKE

Cooking time: $2\frac{1}{2}$ hours   *Quantity:* 4 helpings

$1\frac{1}{2}$ lb haricot beans
salt and pepper
1 lb firm mashed potatoes
4 oz fat boiled bacon

2 teaspoons dried sage
1 teaspoon sugar
crisp breadcrumbs

METHOD: Soak the haricot beans for 24 hours, then simmer them for $1\frac{1}{2}$ hours in enough salted water to keep them covered. Mash beans thoroughly, mix with potato, chopped bacon, sage, pepper and sugar. If the paste seems stiff, add a little bean water.

Grease a cake tin, sprinkle the sides and bottom with the breadcrumbs, press the mixture into the tin, cover with a greased paper and bake in a moderate oven for 1 hour. Serve with cabbage or Brussels sprouts and brown gravy.

Give them Beans

Look ahead to next winter, and plant beans now. Haricots are the best kind. You'll be glad to have a store of them. They are fine food, and a clever cook can work wonders with them.

FOOD FACTS

OATMEAL DOWN IN PRICE! Thanks to the Government subsidy, loose oatmeal and rolled oats (oat flakes) cost today only 3½d per lb. or less.

THERE are *3* good reasons why you should eat plenty of oatmeal. First, for fitness; oatmeal gives you energy, helps to protect you from illness, and makes strong bones and healthy blood. Secondly, it is home-produced. Thirdly, it is economical; you can add it to almost every kind of dish to make it go further and increase its food value. Here you will find a few suggestions.

Oatmeal Flour

Mix your week's supply of flour with a quarter of the bulk of oatmeal; this will add to its flavour and make it more wholesome. You will not need quite so much fat with it either. *Remember, though, oatmeal contains fat and will keep only a few weeks.*

Oatmeal for soups and stews

Thicken your soups and stews with oatmeal. It will give them a delicious flavour and greatly increase their nourishment.

Oatmeal Mince

Mince 1 lb skirt of beef. Toast ¼ lb coarse oatmeal in the oven until it is crisp and nutty. Add it to the beef with salt and pepper and a grated carrot, and mix well. Moisten with water or stock. Cook in a covered casserole in a low oven for 2½–3 hours.

OATMEAL STUFFING

This is particularly useful for making meat, fish or poultry go further.

Boil 3 oz coarse oatmeal in 1½ teacups water for 30 minutes. Mix well with 2 oz breadcrumbs, salt and pepper, 1 teaspoon mixed sweet herbs, 1 teaspoon chopped parsley, 1 grated onion (if you can get it) and a pinch of mace if liked. Bind with a little melted dripping if necessary.

OATMEAL SAUSAGES

Cooking time: 30 minutes   *Quantity:* 4 helpings

2 tablespoons chopped onion or leek
½ oz cooking fat or dripping
4 oz oatmeal
½ pint water

2 teaspoons salt
¼ teaspoon pepper
2 oz chopped meat or sausage or bacon
browned breadcrumbs

METHOD: Fry the onion or leek in the fat or dripping until lightly browned. Work in the oatmeal, add the water gradually and bring to the boil, stirring all the time. Cook for 10–15 minutes, stirring frequently. Add the seasoning and chopped meat or sausage or bacon, mix well and spread on a plate to cool. Divide into 8 portions and roll into sausage shapes. (These may be prepared the previous day). Coat with browned crumbs and either fry in a little hot fat or grill.

HUNT PIE

Cooking time: 35 minutes
Ingredients: $\frac{3}{4}$ to 1 pint of water (in which lentils soaked), 2 oz chopped leek, $\frac{3}{4}$ lb chopped root vegetables and cabbage, 4 oz lentils (soaked overnight), 2 oz minced meat, $\frac{1}{2}$ teaspoon meat or vegetable extract, salt and pepper. **Pastry:** 2 oz oatmeal, 2 oz flour, 1 level teaspoon baking powder, water to mix, salt, 1 dessertspoon chopped mint and parsley. **Quantity:** 4 helpings

Bring water to boil, add leek, vegetables, lentils, meat extract, seasoning. Put on pan lid, cook for 10 to 15 minutes, stir to prevent sticking. Make pastry, press into a round, place on top of the meat, vegetables etc. Replace lid. Cook for a further 15–20 minutes. Lift pastry with a slice, slide meat, etc, into a dish, put pastry on top, sprinkle with chopped parsley and mint. Serve with mashed potatoes and watercress.

PIGS IN CLOVER

For this wholesome and economical dish you will need 6 medium, well-scrubbed potatoes, 6 skinned sausages and some cabbage. With an apple corer, remove a centre core lengthways from each potato and stuff the cavity with sausage meat. Bake the potatoes in the usual way and serve on a bed of lightly chopped, cooked cabbage.

A meaty subject...

She needs as much meat as he does!

Do heavy workers need more meat?
No. Daily wear and tear on the tissues is not materially affected by the kind of work done.

STEAK AND VEGETABLE RAGOÛT

Cooking time: $2\frac{1}{4}$ hours   *Quantity:* 4 helpings

1 lb root vegetables in season	1 breakfastcup of previously soaked dried peas or beans
a little fat	
1 lb stewing steak in one piece	salt and pepper
	water

METHOD: Prepare and fry the vegetables in a little fat. Fry the meat on both sides lightly. Cut some of the meat into small pieces, leaving a good shaped piece of the meat 'solid'. Place all in a saucepan with the peas or beans, seasoning and water. Simmer gently for about 2 hours. Take out the large piece of meat and serve the rest as a stew. Part of the main piece of meat can be sliced and warmed up with hot gravy for other meals.

'For only 12 points you can get a lovely big tin of American pork sausagemeat' says Mrs Merry, 'But what's the best way to use it?'

There's lots of ways to use it, but here's one of our favourites and the beautiful clean pork fat in the tin is wonderful for making pastry.

FILLETS OF PORK

METHOD Flake $\frac{1}{2}$ lb pork sausagemeat (with the outside fat removed), then mix in $\frac{1}{2}$ lb mashed potatoes and one cupful of crisp breadcrumbs. Season well with pepper and salt adding a pinch of sage if liked. Then bind with a thick sauce made from the meat juices taken from the can, and made up to 1 teacup measure with vegetable stock and 1 tablespoon flour plus a little of the pork fat from the tin.

Divide into nine or ten sections, shape into finger rolls, coat in more crumbs, and fry or bake till heated through and crisp-coated, with a light greasing of pork fat for the frying pan or baking tin.

These are delicious by themselves, or served with Leek Sauce.

MINCE SLICES

Cooking time: 5 to 7 minutes   *Quantity:* 4 helpings

8 oz mince (any cooked meat)
4 oz cooked mashed potatoes

4 oz stale breadcrumbs
salt and pepper
fat, optional

METHOD: Mix well together the mince, mashed potatoes, breadcrumbs and salt and pepper. Turn out on floured board and roll into an oblong $\frac{1}{4}$ inch thick. Cut into slices and fry in a small quantity of hot fat, or grill for 5 to 7 minutes. Serve with leek sauce, mashed potatoes and a green vegetable.

SAVOURY MEAT ROLL

Cooking time: 2 hours   *Quantity:* 4 helpings

4 oz stale bread
$\frac{3}{4}$ lb sausage meat
5 oz pinto beans, cooked and mashed
pepper and salt

1 teaspoon made mustard
1 teaspoon thyme
gravy browning
browned breadcrumbs

METHOD: Soak the stale bread in water until soft. Squeeze out the water and mash the bread with the sausage meat, the mashed beans, pepper, salt, made mustard and thyme. Add gravy browning until the mixture is a rich brown. Press very firmly into a greased 2 lb stone jam jar or tin, and steam for 2 hours. Roll in browned breadcrumbs and serve hot with brown gravy, or cold with a raw cabbage heart salad and boiled potatoes.

LEEK SAUCE

Cooking time: 25 minutes **Ingredients:** $\frac{1}{2}$ pint milk and water, half a leek chopped, salt and pepper, 1 oz flour, pinch of herbs. **Quantity:** 4 helpings

Put some of the milk, or milk and water, leek and seasoning into a pan and allow to simmer slowly for 15 to 20 minutes. Blend the flour with the remaining cold milk, stir into the pan with the leek, etc and cook for a minute or two.

SCOTCH EGGS

Cooking time: 30 minutes   *Quantity:* 2–4 helpings

2 reconstituted dried eggs
8 oz sausagemeat

little flour
crisp breadcrumbs

METHOD: Hardboil the eggs as the instruction on page 69 then coat them with the sausagemeat. Form into neat shapes, dust with flour, then roll in breadcrumbs. Bake on a greased tin in the centre of a moderate oven.
Note: If you can spare an extra reconstituted dried egg coat the sausagemeat with this (or part of the egg) before coating with the breadcrumbs. When you have any fat to spare fry the Scotch Eggs instead of baking them.

BRISKET OF BEEF

Cooking time: 2¼ hours   *Quantity:* 4 helpings

1 lb mixed vegetables
   (carrots, turnips, parsnips)
¼ lb stewing steak
a level tablespoon national
   flour or oatmeal

salt and pepper
a knob of dripping or
   margarine
potatoes

METHOD: Wash and cut up vegetables. Cut meat into small pieces and dip in flour or oatmeal, salt and pepper mixed together. Heat fat in a large saucepan, brown meat on both sides, take it out, and put in layer of vegetables. Put back the meat, cover with the rest of the vegetables, and add boiling water to cover. Put on pan lid, simmer for 2 hours. Put in scrubbed potatoes half an hour before serving.

BAKED STEAK WITH SLICED POTATOES

METHOD: Scrub and cut into ½ in thick slices, 2 lb potatoes. Parboil 10 minutes in salted water. Put half into a greased baking tin with a little sliced onion. Add 1 lb piece of stewing steak, cut thick, on top of this put a 'blanket' of sausage-meat, shaped to fit the steak. Cover with the rest of the potato slices. Thicken ½ pint of the potato liquid with a teaspoon each of gravy powder and flour; pour it on. Bake in a moderate oven 1 to 1½ hours. When half-cooked, brush the top potatoes with dripping and sprinkle with salt.

MEAT ROLL

First of all soak a large slice of bread in milk. Now mix together ¼ lb minced veal, ¼ lb minced beef, ¼ lb sausage meat and a few minced bacon pieces. Add to them a small onion or one or two spring onions (if you can get them) sliced finely, a grated raw potato and salt and pepper to taste. Squeeze the milk out of the slice of bread and mash the bread into the meat mixture. If you can spare it, bind the mixture with a small beaten egg; otherwise use the milk in which the bread was soaked. If necessary, add enough white breadcrumbs to make the mixture firm enough to shape into a roll. Sprinkle thickly with browned breadcrumbs or medium oatmeal that has been toasted in the oven, put into a greased baking tin, cover with butter or margarine paper and bake in a good oven for an hour.

This roll can be served hot or cold. It looks most attractive when decorated with strips of anchovy or some sliced, cooked carrot sprinkled with a little chopped parsley.

SPICED BEEF

3 to 4 lb boneless brisket or rolled thin flank. Mix together 1 teaspoonful each sugar, made mustard, salt, 2 tablespoonfuls vinegar and rub well into the meat, all over with back of a wooden spoon. Leave meat in dish, with 2 bayleaves, 4 cloves, $\frac{1}{2}$ teaspoon peppercorns, for about 12 hours. Turn occasionally. Put the meat, with all its juices and spices into a pan, add 2 small onions (home pickled ones do nicely) sliced, and $\frac{1}{2}$ lb sliced carrots and small bunch parsley. Just cover with water, put on lid and simmer slowly for 3 hours. The meat may be served hot, with the liquid thickened as gravy, or placed between two plates with a weight on top and left to get cold, the thickened liquid served as a cold sauce. If the oven is on, the meat can be cooked in a casserole; 4 hours at a very low heat.

LANCASHIRE HOT POT

Cooking time: 2$\frac{1}{2}$ to 4 hours   *Quantity:* 6 helpings

$\frac{3}{4}$ lb meat
2 carrots, sliced
1 onion or leek, if possible, sliced
3 lb potatoes, peeled and sliced

1 dessertspoon fat from the meat or dripping
$\frac{1}{2}$ pint vegetable stock
1 dessertspoon flour
pepper and salt

METHOD: Cut up meat into small pieces and place in a fireproof dish or casserole. Add sliced carrots and onion or leek, and pepper and salt. Add half the potatoes. Instead of slicing potatoes crack off lumps with a knife. Place the fat from the meat or the dripping on top. Put in a moderate oven with lid on for half an hour. Take out, add stock, blend 1 dessertspoon flour in a little water, pour into casserole. Add remainder of potatoes and sprinkle with salt and pepper. Cook in a moderate oven. Remove the lid for the last 20 minutes and cook until the potatoes are brown.

MACARONI AND BACON DISH

Cooking time: 30 minutes   *Quantity:* 4 helpings

$\frac{1}{2}$ oz dripping or other fat
2 oz leek or onion, peeled and chopped
2 oz bacon, chopped
1 pint stock or water

6 oz macaroni
1 teaspoon salt
pinch pepper
watercress

METHOD: Melt the dripping or fat in a pan and fry the leek or onion and bacon until lightly browned. Add the stock or water and when boiling, add the macaroni and seasoning. Cook for about 20 minutes or until the macaroni is tender and the water is absorbed. Serve very hot garnished with watercress.

PORK PASTIES

METHOD: Chop 1 leek. Place in a saucepan with $\frac{1}{2}$ teaspoon fat cook slowly for ten minutes. Add 1 grated carrot, 6 oz sausagemeat, $\frac{1}{2}$ teacup breadcrumbs and 1 dessertspoon gravy powder, with enough vegetable liquor to loosen. Mix well, then cook slowly for 10 minutes. Season, cool and use as a filling for pasties.

STEAK AND POTATO PIE

Cooking time: 25 minutes   *Quantity:* 4 helpings

8 oz onions, sliced thinly
$\frac{1}{2}$ oz cooking fat or dripping
3 tablespoons flour
$\frac{1}{4}$ pint water
1 tin stewed steak (16 oz size)

1 tin peas (8 oz size)
1 teaspoon salt
$\frac{1}{4}$ teaspoon pepper
2 lb potatoes, cooked and
   mashed

METHOD: Fry the onions gently in the fat or dripping until tender; work in the flour. Add the water gradually and bring to the boil, stirring all the time; boil for 5 minutes. Add the steak, peas and seasoning and mix well. Place the mixture in a pie dish, cover with the mashed potato and brown under the grill or in a hot oven.

BEEF OLIVE PIE

Cooking time: $1\frac{3}{4}$ hours   *Quantity:* 4 helpings

STUFFING
6 oz stale bread, soaked in
   water and then squeezed
   dry
2 tablespoons chopped suet
   or $\frac{3}{4}$ oz fat, melted
2 tablespoons chopped
   parsley
1 tablespoon chopped mixed
   herbs or 1 teaspoon dried
   herbs
1 teaspoon salt
$\frac{1}{4}$ teaspoon pepper
4 tablespoons chopped onion

2 teaspoons lemon juice or
   lemon squash
FILLING AND TOPPING
1 lb stewing steak
$\frac{1}{2}$ oz dripping
$\frac{3}{4}$ oz flour
$\frac{3}{4}$ pint water or stock
1 teaspoon salt
pinch pepper
gravy browning
shortcrust or potato or
   oatmeal pastry made with 6
   oz flour, etc. see pages 52–
   53

METHOD: Mix the ingredients for the stuffing well together. Cut the meat into 8 thin slices about 3 by 4 inches. Spread a little stuffing on each slice of meat and roll up neatly. Make the remainder of the stuffing into about 8 small balls. Pack the olives and balls in a pie dish. Melt the dripping in a saucepan, add the flour and cook for a few minutes until brown. Add the water or stock, bring to the boil, stirring all the time and boil gently for 5 minutes. Season and colour with gravy browning. Pour the gravy into the pie dish. Roll out the pastry and cover the dish. Bake in the centre of a moderate oven for $1\frac{1}{2}$ hours.

RECIPE of the WEEK

BAKED CARROT AND ONION PIE

Cooking time: 45 minutes
Ingredients: $1\frac{1}{2}$ lb carrots, sliced, 6 oz turnips, sliced, 6 oz onion or leek, sliced, 2 oz bacon, chopped, 1 teaspoon salt, $\frac{3}{4}$ pint milk and vegetable stock, see method, $4\frac{1}{2}$ tablespoons flour, pinch pepper, pinch ground nutmeg, 2 slices bread (cut 1 inch thick from a 2 lb loaf), diced, 2 tablespoons melted dripping or margarine. **Quantity:** 4 helpings

Boil the vegetables and bacon in a little salted water until tender. Strain the vegetables and bacon; keep the liquid for the sauce then measure out enough milk to give a total of $\frac{3}{4}$ pint of liquid. Place the cooked vegetables in a pie dish. Blend the flour with a little of the liquid, bring the rest of the liquid to the boil and pour on to the blended flour. Return to the saucepan, stir until it boils and boil gently for 5 minutes. Add the seasoning, pour the sauce over the vegetables in the dish. Cover with the bread and spoon the melted dripping or margarine over the top. Bake in a hot oven for 15–20 minutes until brown and crisp on top.

The Butcher says..

'That's right, Mrs. Smith. We're getting a seventh of our meat now in corned beef—twopence in the 1s. 2d. as you might say. Lord Woolton's watching his stocks—he likes to be sure he's got a bit in hand. I don't mind telling you I was rather afraid the whole ration would be cut down. It's lucky for everyone there is this corned beef to help out with. Cold or hot, you can dish it up in a dozen different ways—and very tasty, too. No, Mrs. Smith, I don't want any points coupons, it's all part of the meat ration.'

CORNED BEEF MOULD

Preparation time: 15 minutes
Ingredients: 2 to 4 oz corned beef, 4 oz soaked bread, 6 oz mashed carrot, mock horse-radish (4 tablespoons shredded swede, 1½ teaspoons mustard, 1½ tablespoons vinegar), chopped parsley, pepper and salt. **Quantity:** 4 helpings

Mix all the ingredients together. Press into basin and leave with plate and weight on top for about 4 hours. Turn out, cut into slices and serve with potato salad and watercress.

AMERICAN MINCE

Cooking time: 30–35 minutes *Quantity:* 4 helpings

6 oz corned beef, minced or finely chopped
8 oz cooked pearl barley
½ pint tomato pulp or white sauce, see page 69
1 teaspoon salt

¼ teaspoon pepper
1 oz cheese, grated
1 oz breadcrumbs
½ oz dripping or margarine
2 tomatoes (if available)

METHOD: Place the beef, barley, tomato pulp or white sauce, seasoning, cheese and breadcrumbs in layers in a greased pie dish. Finish with a layer of cheese and dot with the dripping or margarine. Bake in a moderate oven for 25 minutes. Slice the whole tomatoes and spread over the top. Return to the oven for a further 5–10 minutes.

CORNED BEEF WITH CABBAGE

AMERICAN CORNED BEEF HASH

Cooking time: 10–15 minutes   *Quantity:* 4 helpings

½ oz cooking fat
1 leek, sliced
1 lb corned beef, cut into
small pieces
1 lb cooked potatoes, cut into
small pieces

1 dessertspoon flour
½ small cup vegetable water
little made mustard, optional
1 cabbage, shredded
salt

Cooking time: 50 minutes. Mix together 1 breakfastcup of chopped corned beef with the same quantity of diced raw potatoes and season with pepper. Put into a frying pan ½ teacup of vegetable water and a teaspoon or two of cooking fat or dripping. When the pan is hot put in the corned beef and potatoes, spreading them evenly. Dot with another teaspoon or two of fat over the top. Place a plate over the pan and cook quite slowly for about 45 minutes. A thick delicious crust will form on the bottom. Fold across and serve on a hot dish with cooked green vegetables. Pickled beetroot or cabbage is excellent with this dish.
NOTE: The pancake on page 36 is similar to this but uses cooked potatoes.

METHOD: Heat the fat in a stout saucepan, add the leek and fry lightly. Put in the corned beef and potatoes, sprinkle with the flour and add the vegetable water with the mustard (if liked). Stir all together until very hot. Meanwhile cook the cabbage in a very little salted water with the lid on the pan. Drain and serve on a hot dish, topped with the meat mixture.

HARICOT BEEF

Cooking time: 1 hour 45 minutes   *Quantity:* 4 helpings

8 oz haricot beans
1 lb corned beef, sliced
1 small cabbage, finely
shredded (if available)
1 leek, chopped
few peppercorns

little salt
1 dessertspoon mustard
powder
1 tablespoon gravy
thickening
½ pint vegetable stock

METHOD: Soak the beans in water to cover for 24 hours then cook for 1 hour and strain. Put the beans, corned beef, cabbage and leek in layers in a dish, with the peppercorns and salt sprinkled between. Add the mustard and gravy thickening with the stock. Cover and cook in a slow oven for 45 minutes.

CORNED BEEF RISSOLES

Cooking time: 20 minutes   *Quantity:* 2–3 helpings

4 oz corned beef
½ lb mashed potatoes
½ lb cooked mixed vegetables
4 oz wheatmeal breadcrumbs

seasoning
pinch mixed herbs
4 tablespoons brown sauce or
vegetable water

METHOD: Flake the corned beef and mix with the mashed cooked vegetables and breadcrumbs. Season and add the mixed herbs. Bind the mixture with sauce or vegetable water, form into shapes. Bake in a quick oven.

Let's talk about WARMING FOOD

It isn't only hot meals that warm; although, of course, they are very comforting. There are foods that stoke your inner fires and, happily, three of the chief of them are cheap and easy to get. They are potatoes, oatmeal (soon to become more plentiful), national wheatmeal bread. These are also important health-protectors. Carrots, too, have some warmth-giving value, and they protect against colds and chills. Carrots also help you to see in the dark.

CORNED BEEF FRITTERS

Cooking time: 10 minutes   *Quantity:* 4 helpings

2 oz self-raising or plain flour
pinch salt
1 egg yolk or ½ reconstituted
   egg
½ gill milk or milk and water
pinch dried mixed herbs

1 teaspoon grated onion
1 teaspoon chopped parsley
6 oz corned beef, finely
   flaked
1 oz clarified dripping or
   cooking fat

METHOD: Blend the flour with the salt, egg and milk or milk and water. Beat until smooth batter then add the herbs, onion, parsley and corned beef. Melt the dripping or fat in a frying pan and when really hot drop in spoonfuls of the batter mixture. Fry quickly on either side until crisp and brown. Serve as soon as possible after cooking.

SAGE AND MINCE PUDDING

Cooking time: 1½ hours **Ingredients:** Mix together 8 oz self-raising flour (or plain flour with 2 teaspoons baking powder), 1 lb grated raw carrots, 3 oz minced stewing steak, 2 tablespoons packet sage and onion stuffing, 1 finely chopped onion, 2 oz melted dripping or fat and seasoning to taste. This should form a stiff dough, but if too dry a little water may be added.

Grease a 2 pint basin, put in the mixture. Cover with a cloth or margarine papers and steam or boil for 1½ hours. Serve with green vegetables and a good gravy. **Quantity:** 4 helpings

POTATO AND CORNED BEEF PANCAKE

When you are offered corned beef instead of your cut of meat, do you know how to make it into a substantial dish? The great point is to keep it moist and utilise its fat to the best advantage. Here is a suggestion from America.

Mix lightly 1 breakfastcup of chopped corned beef with the same quantity of diced cooked potatoes, and season with pepper and salt. Pour into a pan ¾ to 1 gill milk or household stock and a teaspoon or so of clarified fat or dripping. When warmed turn in the meat and potatoes, spreading them evenly. Flick another two teaspoons of fat over the top. Place a plate over the pan and allow the pancake to cook quite slowly for about half an hour. A thick delicious crust will form on the bottom. Fold the pancake across and serve it up on a hot dish with sprouts or any other cooked green vegetable.

SAUSAGES AND BEANS

Cooking time: 15–20 minutes   *Quantity:* 4 helpings

1 tin sausages (16 oz size)
1 tin beans in tomato sauce
   (16 oz size)
2 teaspoons mustard powder

2 teaspoons sugar
1 tablespoon bottled sauce*
1 tablespoon vinegar
1 lb potato, mashed

METHOD: Remove and keep the fat from around the tinned sausages; slice the sausages. Mix together the beans, mustard, sugar, sauce and vinegar and place in a shallow ovenproof dish. Cover with the sliced sausages and surround with mashed potato. Dot the potato with a little of the sausage fat and bake in a hot oven for 15–20 minutes or until brown.

*Use Worcester sauce or one similar in flavour.

CORNED BEEF HASH

METHOD: Peel and grate 2 medium onions, dice 8 oz corned beef and 8 oz cooked potatoes, slice 8 oz tomatoes. Melt $\frac{1}{2}$ oz dripping in a strong frying pan. Add the onions and fry gently until soft. Add the corned beef and potatoes, cook for several minutes, then add the tomatoes and a little seasoning. Cover the pan with a plate and cook very slowly for 15 minutes.

CURRIED CORNED BEEF BALLS

Cooking time: 10 minutes   *Quantity:* 4 helpings

$\frac{1}{2}$ oz dripping or fat
1 tablespoon grated onion
1 teaspoon curry powder
6 oz corned beef, finely diced

$\frac{1}{2}$ teacup soft breadcrumbs
$\frac{1}{2}$ teaspoon Worcester sauce
little milk
$\frac{1}{2}$ teacup crisp breadcrumbs

METHOD: Heat the dripping or fat and fry the onion for 5 minutes. Stir in the curry powder, cook for 2 minutes with the onion, stirring well, then add the corned beef, soft breadcrumbs and Worcester sauce. Press the mixture into small balls, brush with the milk then roll in the crisp breadcrumbs. Either serve cold or heat under the grill, or in the oven if this is in use.

QUESTIONS YOU ASK

My packed lunches are so monotonous. Can you suggest something for a change?

We think you will like Bacon Turnovers.

BACON TURNOVERS (2)

Grill 4 oz fat bacon rashers until the fat is brown and well frizzled. Pour off the liquid fat and set aside to get cold and congealed. When quite cold treat as lard. Rub it into 8 oz self-raising flour (or plain flour with 2 teaspoons baking powder). Season with pepper. Mix to a soft dough with water. Roll out and cut into rounds. Finely dice 8 oz cooked mixed vegetables, mince the grilled bacon, mix with the vegetables. Moisten with a little gravy. Put a spoonful of the mixture into the centre of each round, fold over, seal the edges, brush

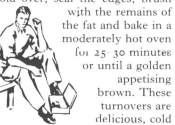

with the remains of the fat and bake in a moderately hot oven for 25–30 minutes or until a golden appetising brown. These turnovers are delicious, cold or hot. See also page 26.

Vegetable Dishes

Home-grown vegetables were a very important part of our diet. We were encouraged to eat plenty of potatoes in place of bread, which used imported wheat, and for the valuable vitamins they contain. Carrots, parsnips and swedes were all used in a variety of recipes and green vegetables were very important and great emphasis was placed on cooking them correctly.

The Greengrocer says ..

RECIPE of the WEEK

CARROT-CAP SALAD

Every woman who values her good complexion should have this salad regularly.

Cook two or three good sized potatoes in their skins. When tender, strain without drying off to avoid making them floury. Slice and dice neatly; then dress in vinaigrette dressing (two parts of salad oil to one of vinegar, pepper and salt to taste) while they are still hot. Pile in a salad bowl lined with a few shredded lettuce leaves or water-cress. Sprinkle with a little chopped chives or rings of spring onion and pile high with grated carrot. To make a more substantial dish, add one or two boned sardines or fillets of smoked herring.

What about some nice carrots this morning? There's a grand crop this year—thanks to the farmers. They do say that for keeping illness at a distance the carrot's a real blessing to all of us, young and old alike. Worth remembering this time of year. And they taste a treat, in my opinion, if you cook 'em cleverly and dish 'em nicely—my missus knows a dozen different ways. Even put them into puddings you can—and very good puddings they make too: you'd be surprised.

POTATO PANCAKE

Cooking time: 10–15 minutes   *Quantity:* 4 helpings

1 lb cooked potatoes
¼ lb sausage meat
1 dessertspoon mint and
   parsley chopped together

1 dessertspoon mixed herbs
salt and pepper
milk
½ oz dripping

METHOD: Mash the potato with the sausage meat, add herbs, seasoning and milk to make a soft mixture. Heat dripping and spread potato mixture to cover the bottom of the pan. Fry until brown and crisp.

SCALLOPED POTATOES (1)

Cooking time: ¾ hour   *Quantity:* 4 helpings

2 lb potatoes
2 tablespoons flour
1 pint milk and water or
   household milk

4–6 oz grated cheese
salt and pepper
2 tablespoons coarsely
   chopped parsley

METHOD: Scrape potatoes and cut into thin slices, blend flour with the milk, arrange potatoes in layers in a pie-dish, sprinkling each layer thickly with cheese, season with salt and pepper, moisten with milk. Finish with a layer of cheese, pour over the remaining milk and cover with a lid or greased paper. Bake in a moderate oven for ¾ hour. Sprinkle with 2 tablespoons of chopped parsley, serve with green vegetables or salad.

The Radio Doctor Says:

'You may have heard what the greengrocer said when a critical customer asked if his vegetables contained vitamins. "If they do," he said, "they can easily be washed off." Well, they *can't* be washed off, but they *can* be cooked out, and that's a form of wastage.'

Song of Potato Pete

Potatoes new, potatoes old
Potato (in a salad) cold
Potatoes baked or mashed or
   fried
Potatoes whole, potato pied
Enjoy them all, including chips
Remembering spuds don't come
   in ships!

POTATO JANE

BAKED POTATOES

When you have the oven on for baking day pop in some potatoes too. Bake in a moderate oven for 45 minutes. When they break under gentle pressure they are ready.

Cooking time: 45 minutes to 1 hour   *Quantity:* 4 helpings

1½ lb potatoes
½ leek, chopped
2 oz breadcrumbs

3 oz cheese, grated
salt and pepper
½–¾ pint of milk

METHOD: Put a layer of sliced potatoes in a fire-proof dish. Sprinkle with some of the leek, crumbs, cheese and seasoning. Fill dish with alternate layers, finishing with a layer of cheese and crumbs. Pour over the milk and bake in a moderate oven for 45 minutes, or steam in a basin for 1 hour. Serve with a raw vegetable salad.

POTATO FINGERS

METHOD: Mix 1 oz flour with $\frac{1}{2}$ lb mashed potato, season with salt and pepper. Bind, if necessary, with a little milk, or reconstituted dried egg. Shape into fingers, glaze with egg or milk, bake in a hot oven for about 10 minutes until brown and crisp.

POTATO FLODDIES

These are real energy givers.

Scrub 2 potatoes and grate with a coarse grater over a bowl. Then add sufficient flour to form a batter. Season with salt and pepper. Melt a little dripping and make very hot in a frying pan. Drop the mixture into it. When brown on one side, turn and brown on the other. Serve with a little jam if you want it as a sweet dish. If you want it as a savoury, add a pinch of mixed herbs and a dash of cayenne pepper.

POTATO BASKET

Scrub 1 lb potatoes and boil gently in a very little water. When they are nearly cooked, drain off the liquid reserving it for stock. Let them finish cooking in their own steam by covering them closely with a folded cloth under the lid and standing the saucepan at the side of the stove until they are floury. Peel and mash well. Add a beaten egg and mash again. Grease a cake tin and coat it with browned breadcrumbs. Press in the mashed potatoes to form a thick lining to the tin. Bake in a hot oven for about 10 minutes. Meanwhile dice 1 lb carrots, having cooked them for 15 minutes, and mix them with a sauce made from 1 oz dripping, 1 oz oatmeal and $\frac{1}{2}$ pint milk or stock, and salt and pepper to taste. When the potato basket is cooked turn it out and fill it with the hot carrot mixture. Heat in the oven for a few minutes and serve piping hot. Enough for 4.

POTATO CARROT PANCAKE

Well-seasoned mashed potato combined with cooked carrot makes a wholesome and savoury tasting pancake. Whip the mashed potato to a loose creamy consistency. Season well with pepper and salt and add some diced cooked carrots. Pan-fried slowly in a very little fat it develops a deliciously crisp crust, but it can be baked to a good brown in the oven if preferred.

CHAMP

METHOD: Cook 2 lb potatoes allowing them to steam off and dry in the usual way. Cook 1 lb green vegetables in a very little water with the lid on the pan. If cabbage is chosen, shred it finely with a knife before cooking. Mash the potatoes with 1 teacup hot milk, beating well until quite smooth, then add the cooked vegetable and season with salt and pepper. Serve piping hot on hot plates with a pat of margarine on each portion

SCALLOPED POTATOES (2)

METHOD: Scrub and scrape 1 lb potatoes, then cut them into fairly thin slices. Arrange in layers in a pie-dish or casserole, sprinkling each layer with flour seasoned with salt and pepper, and sliced spring onion. Pour over $\frac{1}{2}$ pint milk, sprinkle the top with breadcrumbs and bake in a moderate oven for about one hour, or cook in a frying-pan covered with a plate for $\frac{1}{2}$ to $\frac{3}{4}$ hour over low heat.

Home-guards of health

Of course you don't want to be a food crank. But it is useful to know that there are certain homely foods that can do a marvellous job of protecting you and your family against illness.

Enlist these 'home guards' in your diet, and keep them regularly on duty!

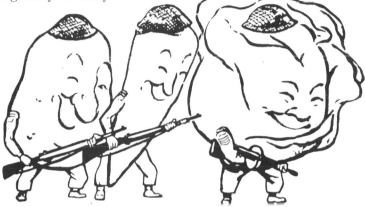

Here are a few simple exercises:

1 Serve a good big helping of any green vegetables every day. Greens should be cooked quickly; served at once; keeping hot or warming up lessens their value.

2 Serve, also, a good portion of root vegetables. Be sure that carrots are served several times a week. When cooking potatoes, boil or steam them in their skins for utmost health value.

3 Give something raw and green every day. Sometimes it may be a salad of shredded cabbage heart or other tender greenstuff; or watercress or mustard-and-cress for tea; or plenty of chopped parsley in a sauce, on potatoes, or in a salad.

PARSLEY POTATO CAKES

METHOD: Boil an extra pound of potatoes the day before you want to make the cakes. Mash these while hot, with a little milk. Season with salt and pepper.

Next day add a tablespoonful or two of chopped parsley and shape the mixture into little cakes. Cover these with brown breadcrumbs, and pan-fry in a little hot fat, or bake in the oven. The mixture should not be made wet. Serves 4 people.

| | QUESTIONS YOU ASK |

My skin is not as good as it used to be; I think it's lack of fruit.

It's the Vitamin C in the fruit that is so good for your skin—and for your health. But you get exactly the same vitamin in vegetables. Remember, however, that you must have *extra* vegetable to make up for the missing fruit. Everyone needs at least 1,000 units of Vitamin C every day. Here is a brief list to guide you.

		Vitamin C Units
	cooked	
Spinach	4 oz	700
Broccoli	,,	600
Turnip Tops	,,	480
Cabbage	,,	300
Swedes	,,	260
Potatoes	,,	240
	raw	
Watercress	½ oz	150
Spinach	,,	150
Cabbage	,,	100
Parsley	,,	70

Note how much richer in Vitamin C are raw vegetables

Then there are carrots. Although not a good source of Vitamin C, carrots provide other elements which clear the skin and improve its texture. A good plan therefore—and a plan for everyone who values health—is to have a raw vegetable salad (based on shredded cabbage heart or other green stuff, watercress and grated carrot); or cooked carrots, or an extra helping of green vegetables *as well as* your usual vegetables, every day.

MARROW SURPRISE

Cooking time: 20 minutes   *Quantity:* 4 helpings

1 medium marrow
8 oz carrots, sliced
1 cup runner beans, sliced
salt
CHEESE SAUCE
1 oz margarine

2 tablespoons flour
½ pint household milk and
  vegetable stock
4 oz cheese, grated
salt and pepper

METHOD: Peel the marrow, unless garden fresh, remove the seeds and cut into large pieces. Put the carrots and beans in a saucepan of boiling salted water. Cover and cook until almost tender. Add the marrow, cook for 5 minutes. Serve with Cheese Sauce.

Melt the margarine in a saucepan, blend in the flour, cook for a few minutes, add the milk and vegetable stock to make a thick sauce, stir until smooth, add the grated cheese and seasoning. Pour the sauce over the marrow, carrots and beans. Brown under the grill. Serve with potatoes.

Save those Orange Rinds!

Here's a new way to make use of orange peel. Grate it and mix a little with mashed potatoes. The potatoes will turn an exciting pink colour.

The Radio Doctor Says:

'For the school child the potato should appear in every midday dinner. It gives energy. The large amounts one eats these days makes them a substantial source of Vitamin C. Potatoes are best steamed or baked in their jackets.

Let the plan be potatoes every day, one or two green vegetables most days, a yellow vegetable, particularly carrot—two or three times a week, and some raw green salad vegetable on most days.

PARSNIP CROQUETTES

Mash 1 lb cooked parsnips with a fork until creamy. Make a thick sauce by melting 1 oz margarine in a saucepan, mixing in smoothly 1 oz flour, cooking together for a minute or two and then adding one small teacup water or vegetable stock in which one teaspoon of vegetable extract has been dissolved. Add 2 teaspoons breadcrumbs and cook for 5 minutes. Add this sauce to the parsnips, and salt and pepper to taste. When cold, divide into 10 or 12 parts and form into croquettes. Roll in browned crumbs or toasted oatmeal. Fry in a very little fat until golden brown on both sides; or form into a large roll, cover well with crumbs and bake in moderate oven for 20 to 30 minutes. Serve hot with gravy, or cold with salad.

CHEESE BEANS

Cooking time: 2 hours   *Quantity:* 4 helpings

½ lb dried beans (soaked
  overnight)
2 oz grated cheese
1 tablespoon vinegar
2 teaspoons Worcester sauce

½ teaspoon made mustard
a good pinch of pepper and
  salt
1 to 2 tablespoons parsley
  and mint, chopped
  together

METHOD: Cook the beans without salt in the water in which they soaked. When the beans are tender, strain and keep two tablespoonfuls of bean water. Add all the other ingredients except herbs to this bean water and cook until cheese is melted. Toss the beans in the cheese sauce, put into a hot dish and sprinkle with chopped parsley and mint. Serve with a green vegetable and potatoes boiled in their skins.

To make Bean Roll, take ½ lb of beans, soak, cook and mash, add the other ingredients as above. Shape into a roll and serve with salad and a little home-made mayonnaise or use as a sandwich filling.

Why is a potato like a lump of sugar?

Because a potato and a lump of sugar are both turned by your digestive system into exactly the same thing — glucose— fuel which your body 'burns' to give you energy and warmth.

Potatoes contain two important health-protecting vitamins and a little body-building material of very good quality.

SCALLOPED VEGETABLES WITH BACON

Cooking time: 30 minutes   *Quantity:* 4 helpings

½ cabbage
3 or 4 carrots
1 leek
4 potatoes or any other
   vegetable
1 oz margarine

2 tablespoons national flour
   or 1 tablespoon fine
   oatmeal
2 or 3 slices bacon
browned bread crumbs

METHOD: Cook vegetables in a pint of water in a closely covered pan. Make thin white sauce with margarine, flour or oatmeal and vegetable water. Arrange vegetables in a fireproof dish, pour sauce over, lay bacon on top, sprinkle with breadcrumbs and crisp under grill.

Cheer up end-of-season potatoes. Boil peeled potatoes in fast boiling salted water with a teaspoonful of vinegar. Mash and cover with chopped parsley and mint or chopped watercress, or chopped carrot tops, or beat in raw vegetables or meat extract, or sprinkle with toasted oatmeal or browned crumbs.

Bake in jackets, split open, cover with grated cheese, return to the oven to brown (or grill for 1–2 minutes).

Cook large potatoes in their skins in boiling salted water. When they show signs of cracking, add cup of cold water; this will drive heat to centre of the potato and hasten cooking.

RECIPE of the WEEK

WARTIME CHAMP

Here is a wartime version of the old Irish dish, Champ. Scrub and slice 1 lb potatoes and 1 lb carrots. Put in a saucepan with a teacupful of hot salted water and add a small cabbage finely shredded. Cover with the lid, cook steadily, giving an occasional shake until tender (about 15 minutes). The water should have just boiled away by then. Add a small teacupful of hot milk and mash well with a dash of pepper and more salt if necessary. Serve at once with a pat of margarine to each helping.

How to keep the Vitamins in the Vegetables

Green vegetables must be cooked as quickly as possible, for slow cooking destroys their valuable vitamins. So always shred them with a knife. Spinach doesn't need shredding as it cooks so quickly.

Never soak green vegetables for a long time. Overlong soaking wastes valuable mineral salts. Just wash the greens thoroughly. But tight-hearted cabbage may be left in salted water for not more than half an hour.

If the outside leaves are too tough to serve, save them for soup. *The dark green leaves have more food value than the centre.*

In cooking green vegetables, use only just enough water to keep the pan from burning—usually a teacupful will do. Spinach needs no added water. Heat the water in the pan before you put in the shredded greens. Next sprinkle with a very little salt. *Now put the lid on the pan*—the greens are going to be 'steam-boiled,' and if it escapes the pan may go dry.

Cook steadily for about 10 to 15 minutes, shaking the pan occasionally. Drain off any liquid from the pan and save it for soup. If you can spare a teaspoon of margarine, add it to the greens and toss well before serving.

TRY THESE FOR A CHANGE

CABBAGE. All sorts of additions may be made to steam-boiled cabbage. A few bacon rinds chopped small; or a few teaspoons of vinegar and a sprinkle of nutmeg or a shake of caraway seeds, and you have something novel and nice.

TOPS. Broccoli tops, turnip tops, and beetroot tops are all excellent if cooked as described above.

RUNNER BEANS. *Young* runner beans should be cooked whole, with just the tops and tails removed.

As a change from slicing the beans, try breaking them with the fingers into inch lengths. This saves a great deal of time and the flavour is better. Steam the broken beans or boil them in a very little salted water until tender (10 to 15 minutes). A teaspoon of fat added to the water makes them glisten and improves the taste.

Cold cooked runner beans are delicious in a salad. Mix a breakfastcup of cooked beans, ready chopped, with a breakfastcup of sliced cooked potatoes and a large lettuce neatly shredded. Decorate with sliced tomatoes or beetroot, nasturtium leaves or parsley.

At the end of the season let the older beans mature on the plant, shell them and dry the inside beans for winter use as haricots.

P's for Protection Potatoes afford;
O's for the Ounces of Energy stored;
T's for Tasty, and Vitamins rich in;
A's for the Art to be learnt in the Kitchen.
T's for Transport we need not demand;
O's for old England's Own Food from the Land;
E's for the Energy eaten by you;
S's for the Spuds which will carry us through!

Potatoes help to protect you from illness. Potatoes give you warmth and energy. Potatoes are cheap and home-produced. So why stop at serving them *once* a day? Have them twice, or even three times—for breakfast, dinner and supper.

STUFFED MARROW

Cooking time: 50 minutes   *Quantity:* 4 helpings

stuffing as in Stuffed
  Cabbage below
1 medium marrow

salt
½ oz cooking fat, melted

METHOD: Peel the marrow and cut lengthways; remove the seeds. Cook in boiling salted water for 5 minutes, drain well. Put the two halves into a tin and fill with the stuffing. Brush with the melted fat. Cover the tin with a lid or greased greaseproof paper. Bake for 45 minutes in a moderate oven. Serve with brown gravy.

STUFFED CABBAGE

Cooking time: 1 hour 5 minutes   *Quantity:* 4 helpings

1 medium cabbage
STUFFING
8 oz sausagemeat
1 onion, grated
4 oz soft breadcrumbs

1 tablespoon chopped parsley
pinch mixed herbs
1 teaspoon Worcester sauce
salt and pepper

METHOD: Put the whole cabbage into boiling salted water and boil for 5 minutes. Remove; retain ½ teacup of the liquid and carefully fold back the leaves, which will by now have softened. Mix all the stuffing ingredients together and put a little of the mixture between the leaves, folding them back as they are filled. Put into a casserole, adding ½ teacup of the vegetable water and covering first with a well greased paper and then the lid. Bake for 1 hour in a moderate oven. To serve, open out the leaves again.

POTATO CHEESE

Cooking time: 25 minutes **Ingredients:** 2 lb old or new potatoes, salt and pepper, 6–8 oz cheese, grated, 2 tablespoons chopped parsley, 2 oz oatmeal. **Quantity:** 4 helpings

Peel or scrub potatoes, cut into small pieces and cook in a small quantity of boiling salted water until soft. Strain and mash in the pan. Mix in half the grated cheese, all the parsley, salt and pepper, turn the mixture into a shallow dish or baking tin, sprinkle the rest of the grated cheese and all the oatmeal over the surface. Put in a moderately hot oven or under a grill to brown. Serve with cabbage (cooked or shredded raw), or spinach.

Bedtime Story

Once upon a time there were five housewives. Their names were Lady Peel-potatoes, the Hon. Mrs. Waste-fuel, Miss Pour-the-vegetable-water-down-the-sink, Mrs. Don't-like-uncooked-vegetables, and Mrs. Won't-eat-carrots. Don't let one of them put a nose in your kitchen.

SAVOURY ONIONS

Cooking time: 1¼ hours   *Quantity:* 4 helpings

4 medium onions
salt and pepper
½ teacup soft breadcrumbs
1 teaspoon chopped sage

2 oz cheese, grated
1 egg or 1 reconstituted egg
½ oz margarine, melted

METHOD: Peel the onions, put into boiling salted water and cook steadily for 30 minutes. Lift the onions out of the liquid, save ½ teacup of this. Remove the centres of the onions, chop this finely and blend with the breadcrumbs, sage, cheese and egg. Season the mixture and fill the onion cases then put these into a casserole with the ½ teacup of onion stock. Brush the onions with the melted margarine. Cover the casserole and bake for 45 minutes in the centre of a moderately hot oven.

BELTED LEEKS

Cooking time: 15 minutes   *Quantity:* 4 helpings

1 lb small leeks
salt and pepper

½ pint white sauce, see page 69
2 oz bacon rashers

METHOD: Prepare the leeks, leave whole and cook in boiling salted water until tender. Drain well, save some of the liquid to make the sauce. Put the leeks in a heated dish and top with the sauce. Grill the bacon, cut into narrow strips. Arrange as 'belts' over the leeks.

TURNIP TOP SALAD

Preparation time: 15 minutes   *Quantity:* 4 helpings

4 oz turnip tops
4 oz white cabbage heart
2 oz raw beetroot

2 oz raw carrots
salad dressing
watercress for garnishing

METHOD: Grate or shred all the vegetables separately and arrange attractively on a large dish. Sprinkle with salad dressing and decorate with watercress. Make the salad dressing by adding vinegar, a little mustard, pepper and salt to a white sauce.

DO'S and DON'TS with Vegetables

DO serve swedes when greens are short, or for a change. Of all the root vegetables, swedes are richest in Vitamin C.

DO provide at least one pound of potatoes per head every day, and less bread.

DO cook potatoes in their skins, this prevents their goodness dissolving into the water.

DO serve something green and raw every day.

DON'T soak vegetables, long, their vitamins and minerals seep out into the water.

DON'T throw vegetable water away, use it for soups and sauces.

How about his Fruit Juice, Mother? Remember he's entitled to it under the new scheme.

PATHFINDER PUDDING

Cooking time: 2 hours   *Quantity:* 4–6 helpings

SUET PASTRY
6 oz national flour
$\frac{1}{2}$ teaspoon salt
$\frac{3}{4}$ teaspoon baking powder
1 oz suet, chopped or grated
$1\frac{1}{2}$ oz uncooked potato,
   shredded
water

FILLING
2 lb cooked parsnips, diced
4 oz cheese, grated
1 uncooked leek, sliced
$\frac{1}{2}$ teaspoon mustard powder
pepper
1 teaspoon salt

METHOD: Mix the flour, salt and baking powder, add the suet, potato and water to bind. Roll out three quarters of the pastry to line a 2 pint greased basin. Mix the parsnips, cheese, leek, mustard, pepper and salt together. Put into the lined basin. Roll out the remaining quarter of pastry to form a lid. Put this on to the pudding, cover with an upturned saucer or greased greaseproof paper and steam for 2 hours.

SALAD SUGGESTIONS

Well shredded spinach, heart of cabbage, leaves of spring greens, make a delicious salad base. And you've no idea until you try them how tasty young dandelion leaves can be. Choose young leaves, wash, chop finely and mix with any raw shredded root vegetables. A little sugar is a help in this kind of salad. Later on, you can use carrot tops, turnip tops, radish tops, and beetroot tops. The addition of any scraps of cold or 'points' meats, corned beef or fish make your salads still more substantial, nourishing and varied.

STUFFED TOMATOES

Make the best use of fresh tomatoes when these are available. Cut a slice from each tomato, scoop out the pulp. Chop this finely. The quantities given are enough for 8 medium or 4 large tomatoes.

1. Make up $\frac{1}{4}$ pint thick well-seasoned white sauce. Add 2 oz grated cheese, 2 tablespoons chopped parsley and the tomato pulp. Spoon into the tomato cases. Serve cold or bake for 10 minutes in a moderately hot oven.

2. Blend 2 fresh eggs or 2 reconstituted dried eggs with the tomato pulp, 4 tablespoons soft breadcrumbs, 2 tablespoons chopped spring onions and a little seasoning. Spoon into the tomato cases. Bake for 10–15 minutes in a moderately hot oven.

POTATO SALAD

Cooking time: 20 minutes   *Quantity:* 4 helpings

$1\frac{1}{2}$ lb potatoes, old or new
$1\frac{1}{2}$ oz flour
$\frac{1}{2}$ pint milk or milk and water
salt and pepper

1 tablespoon vinegar
1 tablespoon chopped parsley
1 tablespoon chopped mint
4 oz grated cheese

METHOD: Peel potatoes, cut into small pieces, cook in a small quantity of boiling salted water until just barely cooked. If old potatoes are used, cook in their skins and peel when cooked. While potatoes are cooking make the dressing. Blend the flour with a little milk to the consistency of thin cream. Boil the rest of the milk, and when boiling add the blended flour. Stir well over gentle heat till the sauce thickens, then add salt, pepper, vinegar, parsley and mint and $\frac{1}{2}$ to 1 teaspoon of made mustard if you like it.

When the potatoes are cooked and strained, dice and while still hot mix with the dressing. Allow to become quite cold and serve on a bed of lettuce with grated cheese.

Puddings

We found it was much more difficult to make puddings than it had been in the past, but with a little imagination we managed to conjure up appetising ends to the meal. We made good use of seasonal fruits and when cooking these sweetened the fruit with saccharin to save sugar, the crushed tablets were always added to the fruit after it was cooked.

MAKING PASTRY

There are many ways of making pastry that do not use too much fat, include potatoes and oatmeal to give a change of flavour, the recipes are on this page. These foods are home grown and save shipping space. Substitute these pastries in any of the recipes that follow.

I saw three ships a-sailing
But not with food for me
For I am eating home-grown foods
To beat the enemy
And ships are filled with guns instead
To bring us Victory

★ ★ ★

POTATO PASTRY

This is pastry that should be used a great deal as it helps to lighten the flour and makes our rations of fat go much further. Here are two versions.

1 Sift 4 oz self-raising flour with a pinch of salt. Rub in 1½–2 oz cooking fat. Add 4 oz smooth mashed potato. Mix thoroughly then add a little water to bind. Roll out on a floured board and use as ordinary shortcrust pastry. It can be baked in a hot oven. Note: This is a soft pastry.

2 Sift 6 oz self-raising flour with a pinch of salt. Rub in 2–3 oz cooking fat, add 2 oz grated raw potato. Mix well and bind with water. Roll out on a floured board and use as ordinary shortcrust pastry. Bake as above. Note: This has a more interesting flavour than No. 1.

OATMEAL PASTRY

Sift 6 oz self-raising flour with a pinch of salt. Rub in 2–3 oz cooking fat, then add 2 oz rolled oats. Mix with water and use as ordinary shortcrust pastry. Bake as potato pastry above.

BAKEWELL TART

Cooking time: 40 minutes   *Quantity:* 4–6 helpings

shortcrust pastry made with 6 oz flour, etc. as Almond Flan, opposite

FILLING
2 tablespoons jam
2 oz margarine
2 oz sugar
1 teaspoon almond essence

1 egg or 1 reconstituted dried egg
2 oz self-raising flour or plain flour with ½ teaspoon baking powder
2 oz soft breadcrumbs
2 oz soya flour
2 tablespoons milk

METHOD: Make the pastry and line a flan ring on a baking sheet or a pie plate or sandwich tin. Spread with the jam. Cream the margarine, sugar and essence together; beat in the egg then add the flour or sifted flour and baking powder and remaining ingredients. Bake as the Almond Flan on this page but allow slightly longer cooking time if necessary. Serve hot or cold.

MOCK APRICOT FLAN

METHOD: Line a large 9 inch pie plate or flan dish with shortcrust pastry or oatmeal pastry or potato pastry, see recipes left and right. Bake without a filling in a hot oven for 20–25 minutes until firm and golden.

Meanwhile grate 1 lb young carrots. Put into a saucepan with a few drops of almond essence, 4 tablespoons of plum jam and only about 4 tablespoons of water. Cook gently until a thick pulp. Spoon into the cooked pastry. Spread with a little more plum jam if this can be spared.

Note: The carrots really do taste a little like apricots.

ALMOND FLAN

Cooking time: 35 minutes   *Quantity:* 4–6 helpings

SHORTCRUST PASTRY
6 oz self-raising flour or plain flour with 1½ teaspoons baking powder
pinch salt
1½–2 oz cooking fat or margarine
water to mix
FILLING
1–2 tablespoons jam

1 oz margarine
1½ oz sugar
1 teaspoon almond essence
1 egg or 1 reconstituted dried egg
1½ oz plain flour
1 teaspoon baking powder
1½ oz semolina
½ teacup milk or milk and water

METHOD: Sift the flour or flour and baking powder and salt. Rub in the cooking fat or margarine, add enough water to make a firm rolling consistency. Roll out and line a flan ring on a baking sheet or a pie plate or sandwich tin; spread with the jam. Cream the margarine, sugar and essence together, beat in the egg. Sift the flour and baking powder. Stir into the creamed mixture, then add the semolina and blend in the milk or milk and water. Spoon into the pastry case. Bake in the centre of a moderately hot oven for 35 minutes or until firm, reduce the heat slightly towards the end of the cooking time if the pastry or filling is becoming too brown. Serve hot or cold.

BRETON PEARS

Cooking time: ½ hour. Make shortcrust pastry using 12 oz self-raising flour, pinch salt, 3 oz cooking fat and water to mix. Roll out and cut into 4 squares. Peel 4 ripe firm pears, take out as much core as possible with a sharp knife and fill the space with some kind of jam, apricot is particularly good. Place the pears on the pastry. Brush the edges of the pastry with water and seal these firmly around the pears. Bake in the centre of a moderately hot oven for 30–35 minutes.

PRUNE FLAN

Cooking time: 1¼ hours   *Quantity:* 4–6 helpings

6 oz prunes, soaked overnight in water to cover
1 tablespoon golden syrup
½ teaspoon ground cinnamon
½ teaspoon mixed spice
1 oz margarine

few drops lemon essence
2 tablespoons soft breadcrumbs
shortcrust pastry made with 6 oz flour, etc, see above

METHOD: Simmer the prunes until tender then lift from the water, cut the fruit into small pieces. Put into a saucepan with all the ingredients, except the pastry and stir over a low heat until well mixed. Allow to cool. Roll out the pastry, line a flan ring or a baking sheet or a pie plate or tin. Put in the prune mixture and bake in the centre of a moderately hot oven for 30 minutes. Serve hot or cold.

The liquid left from soaking the prunes can be thickened and served with the flan.

CAKE OR PUDDING MIXTURE

Cooking time: 20 minutes or 1 hour   *Quantity:* 4 helpings

1 egg (1 level tablespoon of dried egg mixed with a tablespoon of water)
2 oz fat
2 oz sugar

4 oz national flour
½ teaspoon baking powder
a little milk or household milk

METHOD: Beat the egg. Cream fat and sugar, add egg and lastly the flour mixed with the baking powder. Mix to a soft consistency with a little milk. Spread in a tin and bake for 15 to 20 minutes. This mixture can be steamed in a basin for 1 hour and served as a pudding with jam or custard sauce.

★   ★   ★

RECIPE of the WEEK

APPLE AND BLACKBERRY ROLY

Cooking time: 30 minutes
Ingredients: potato pastry as page 52, 1 lb cooking apples, peeled, cored and chopped, ½ lb blackberries, 2 oz sugar. **Quantity:** 4 helpings

Roll the pastry out to an oblong shape. Spread with the apples and blackberries, sprinkle with the sugar and roll up. Seal the ends of the roll, place on a well-greased tin and bake in a moderate oven for 30 minutes.

BEETROOT PUDDING

Here is a new notion for using the sweetness of beetroot to make a nice sweet pudding with very little sugar.

First mix 6 oz wheatmeal flour with ½ teaspoon baking powder. Rub in ½ oz fat and add 1 oz sugar and 4 oz cooked or raw beetroot very finely grated.

Now mix all the ingredients to a soft cake consistency with 3 or 4 tablespoons of milk. Add a few drops of flavouring essence if you have it. Turn the mixture into a greased pie dish or square tin and bake immediately in a moderate oven for 35–40 minutes. This pudding tastes equally good hot or cold. Enough for 4.

STEAMED PUDDINGS

In many of these puddings you will find in some instances a fairly high percentage of rising agent, i.e. baking powder suggested with plain flour. This is because the war-time national flour, while being nutritious, was heavy and needed extra raising agent.

RHUBARB SPONGE

Cooking time: ¾–1 hour   *Quantity:* 4 helpings

1½ lb rhubarb
2 tablespoons golden syrup
1½ oz margarine or cooking fat
3 tablespoons sugar
1 tablespoon dried egg

4 oz self-raising flour or plain flour and 2 teaspoons baking powder
pinch salt
milk or water to mix

METHOD: Wipe the rhubarb and cut into small pieces. Place with the syrup in a pie dish. Cream the margarine or fat and sugar and beat in the egg. Mix the flour or flour and baking powder and salt, add to the creamed mixture alternately with the milk or water to form a dropping consistency. Spread over the fruit and bake in the centre of a moderate oven for ¾–1 hour, depending on whether a shallow or deep pie dish is used.

GLAZED PEARS

Cooking time: $\frac{3}{4}$ to 1 hour **Ingredients:** 6 to 8 firm pears, 1 pint water, 2 good tablespoons raspberry or plum jam, $\frac{1}{2}$ teaspoon vanilla essence, $\frac{1}{2}$ teaspoon almond essence, 1 tablespoon sugar, few drops cochineal, optional, 2 teaspoons arrowroot or cornflour.

Method: This is a very good way to serve pears for one of the meals at Christmas time and British pears should be available. Peel the pears, try and keep them whole. Remove the core, if possible, with the tip of a sharp knife. Put the water, jam, essences and sugar into a saucepan, bring to boiling point. Add the pears and simmer steadily until tender. Keep turning the fruit in the liquid until well coated. Lift out of the liquid and tint this slightly with the cochineal, if you want a deeper colour. Measure the liquid, you should have $\frac{1}{2}$ pint. Blend with the arrowroot or cornflour, return to the pan and stir over the heat until thickened. Spoon over the pears. Serve cold with Mock Cream, recipes on page 61. **Quantity:** 6–8 helpings

PRUNE ROLY

Cooking time: 1 hour   *Quantity:* 4–6 helpings

8 oz national flour
2 teaspoons baking powder
pinch of salt
milk and water for mixing
2 to 4 oz prunes, cooked

2 oz breadcrumbs
1 tablespoon syrup
2 teaspoons sugar
$\frac{1}{2}$ teaspoon cinnamon or spice
1 oz cooking fat

METHOD: Blend flour, baking powder, salt. Mix to a soft consistency with milk and water. Roll out, spread with prunes, breadcrumbs, syrup, sugar and cinnamon. Form into a roll. Melt the fat in a roasting tin and when hot put in the roll, turning it in the fat. Bake for 1 hour in a moderately hot oven.

RHUBARB CRUMBLE

Cooking time: 30 minutes   *Quantity:* 4 helpings

1 lb rhubarb
2 tablespoons golden syrup
$1\frac{1}{2}$ oz fat

4 oz plain flour
pinch salt
3 tablespoons sugar

METHOD: Wipe the rhubarb and cut into small pieces. Simmer with the syrup until cooked and place at the bottom of a fireproof dish. Rub the fat into the flour, salt and sugar until like fine breadcrumbs and sprinkle over the stewed fruit. Bake in a moderate oven for 15–20 minutes.

GINGER PUDDING

Cooking time: $1\frac{1}{2}$ hours   *Quantity:* 4 helpings

6 oz plain flour
2 teaspoons bicarbonate of
  soda
2 teaspoons ground ginger
2 tablespoons sugar

3 oz sultanas or dates,
  chopped
1 oz margarine
$\frac{1}{2}$ pint milk

METHOD: Sift the flour, soda and ginger into a bowl, add the sugar and sultanas or dates. Boil the margarine and milk, pour into the bowl and mix well. Grease a 2 pint basin and put in the mixture, cover with greased, greaseproof paper and steam for $1\frac{1}{2}$ hours. Serve with custard or a sweet sauce.

The Ministry of Food wants your cooking secrets

SPICED COTTAGE PUDDING WITH LEMON SAUCE

Cooking time: 30 minutes   *Quantity:* 4 helpings

8 oz self-raising flour or plain
   flour with 4 teaspoons
   baking powder
pinch salt
2 tablespoons dried egg
3 oz fat

3 oz sugar
1 teaspoon ground cinnamon
½ teaspoon grated nutmeg
½ teaspoon mixed spice
approximately ¼ pint milk

METHOD: Mix the flour or flour and baking powder with the salt and dried egg. Rub the fat in well. Add the sugar with the spices; mix to a stiff consistency with the milk. Turn into a greased Yorkshire pudding tin about 8 × 6 inches. Bake in the centre of a moderately hot oven for 30 minutes. Cut in squares and serve hot with lemon sauce, below.

LEMON SAUCE

Cooking time: 10 minutes   *Quantity:* 4 helpings

8 tablespoons lemon squash
water

3 teaspoons arrowroot
3 tablespoons sugar

METHOD: Make the lemon squash up to 1 pint with the water. Mix the arrowroot and sugar to a cream with a little of the liquid. Bring the rest of the liquid to the boil, pour on to the blended mixture and return to the saucepan. Stir until it comes to the boil and cook for 5 minutes.

PUDDING WITH CEREALS

During the past years several new cereals have made their appearance. With careful cooking, these are very good substitutes for the old familiar ones. Allow 1 oz of cereal per person.

SOYAGHETTI

Cooking time: 2 hours **Ingredients:** 1 pint water, 3 oz soyaghetti, 1 pint milk or milk and water, 1 oz sugar, ½ oz margarine, when possible. **Quantity:** 4–6 helpings

Bring the water to the boil, drop in the soyaghetti and cook for 20 minutes. Strain, if using milk and water in which to bake the soyaghetti, save some of this liquid. Put the cereal in a pie dish, pour over the liquid, add the sugar and margarine. If possible soak for several hours before cooking. Bake for approximately 2 hours in the centre of a very moderate oven. Soyaghetti is probably the best substitute for rice.

Chocolate Soyaghetti:
Ingredients as above but add ½ oz cocoa or 1 oz chocolate powder. Proceed as above.

FARINOCA

Cooking time: 2 hours   *Quantity:* 4–6 helpings

3 oz farinoca
1 pint milk or milk and water

1 oz sugar
½ oz margarine, when possible

METHOD: Put the cereal in the pie dish, pour over the milk or milk and water, add the sugar and margarine. This cereal is undoubtedly better if soaked overnight before baking. When baking, put into the centre or near the bottom of a very moderate oven and cook for 2 hours.
   Farinoca is a good substitute for tapioca.

CARAMEL AND SEMOLINA MOULD

Cooking time: 15 minutes   *Quantity:* 4 helpings

2 oz sugar
4 tablespoons water
1 pint milk or milk and water

1 tablespoon apricot jam or
  marmalade
3 oz semolina

METHOD· Put the sugar and 2 tablespoons of water into a saucepan, stir until the sugar has dissolved, then boil until a golden caramel. Add the remaining water and heat until blended, cool slightly then pour into a basin or mould.

Meanwhile bring the milk or milk and water to the boil in a separate pan, add the jam or marmalade, whisk in the semolina and cook steadily for 10–15 minutes, stirring most of the time. Allow to cool and stiffen slightly, stir briskly then spoon over the caramel and allow to set. Turn out to serve.

EGGLESS SPONGE PUDDING

Cooking time: $1\frac{1}{4}$–$1\frac{1}{2}$ hours   *Quantity:* 4–6 helpings

6 oz self-raising flour or plain
  flour with $1\frac{1}{2}$ teaspoons
  baking powder
$1\frac{1}{2}$–2 oz margarine or cooking
  fat
$1\frac{1}{2}$–2 oz sugar

1 tablespoon golden syrup
$\frac{1}{2}$ teaspoon bicarbonate of
  soda
1 dessertspoon vinegar
milk to mix

METHOD: Sift the flour or flour and baking powder, rub in the margarine or cooking fat, add the sugar and golden syrup. Blend the bicarbonate of soda with the vinegar, add to the other ingredients, with enough milk to make a sticky consistency. Put the mixture into a greased basin, allow room to rise. Cover with a plate or margarine paper. Steam for $1\frac{1}{4}$–$1\frac{1}{2}$ hours or until firm. Serve hot with fruit or jam.

VARIATIONS

A little golden syrup or jam could be put into the basin before adding the sponge mixture.

Chocolate Sponge:

Use 5 oz flour and 1 oz cocoa powder.

VICTORY SPONGE

Grate 1 large raw potato and 2 medium raw carrots, mix in 1 breakfast cup breadcrumbs, 1 tablespoon self-raising flour, 2 tablespoons sugar, $\frac{1}{2}$ teaspoon flavouring, such as vanilla or lemon. Thoroughly stir in 1 teaspoon baking powder. Put 2 or 3 tablespoons of jam in a heated basin, run it round to cover the inside. Cool. Put in the pudding mixture, tie on a cover of margarine paper, steam 2 hours.

Based on Bread

The recipes on this page use bread in interesting ways to make puddings.

POOR KNIGHT'S FRITTERS

Cooking time: few minutes   *Quantity:* 4 helpings

8 large slices of bread
little margarine

jam or golden syrup or thick
   fruit purée
little fat for frying

METHOD: Make sandwiches of the bread, margarine and jam or golden syrup or fruit. Cut into fingers and fry in a little hot fat. You can make nicer fritters if you dip the sandwich fingers into beaten reconstituted dried egg, mixed with a little milk, before frying. Top with sugar.

DANISH APPLE PUDDING

Cooking time: 1 hour   *Quantity:* 4–6 helpings

2 lb apples, peeled and sliced
little water
4 saccharine tablets
few drops almond essence

½ oz margarine, melted
2 teacups breadcrumbs
2 tablespoons golden syrup

METHOD: Cook the apples in a little water until soft. Add the saccharine and almond essence, beat to a pulp with a fork. Grease a pie dish with the margarine. Sprinkle in a layer of crumbs, add a layer of apples. Continue like this until the dish is full, ending with breadcrumbs. Drip the syrup over the top and bake in the centre of a moderate oven for 1 hour.

EVERY CRUMB COUNTS

Never throw away stale bread. Use it as breadcrumbs in savoury or sweet puddings. Bake strips of bread for rusks. Use crisped breadcrumbs as a breakfast cereal, or crush them for coatings. Soak, squeeze and beat up with a fork for sweet and savoury puddings, etc.

CRUMBED PRUNES

Preparation time: 10 minutes   *Quantity:* 4 helpings

1 breakfastcup cooked prunes
1 breakfastcup crisped
   breadcrumbs

1 tablespoon sugar
½ pint thick custard

METHOD: Stone the prunes and cut them into small pieces. Mix with the crumbs and sugar. Put dessertspoons of the custard into individual fruit glasses, then portions of the prunes mixture, and top with custard. The sweet should be served as soon as possible after being prepared, so that the crisp crumbs and sugar contrast with the smoothness of the custard.

We all liked Mrs. Parker, in the City, until we heard she wasted crusts (a pity!).

DUKE PUDDING

Soak 2 breakfastcups stale bread in cold water, squeeze as dry as possible, beat out lumps with a fork. Add 2 tablespoons fat or flaked margarine, 2 tablespoons sugar, 3 tablespoons any dried fruit, small teacup grated raw carrot, 1 teaspoon mixed spice. Stir 1 teaspoon bicarbonate of soda into a little milk and water (milk bottle rinsings will do) and blend well into the mixture. Spread evenly in a greased tart tin, sprinkle with a little sugar, bake in a moderate oven for 30 minutes.

BREAD PUDDING

A Bread Pudding is an excellent way to use up bread. The recipe below can be varied in many ways, for example if you are short of dried fruit use a diced cooking apple or a little more marmalade. Slices of Bread Pudding are ideal to tuck into a packed meal box for a factory worker.

Cooking time: $1\frac{1}{2}$ or 2 hours   *Quantity:* 4 helpings

8 oz stale bread
2 oz grated suet or melted
   cooking fat
1 oz sugar
1 tablespoon marmalade

2 oz dried fruit
1 reconstituted dried egg
milk to mix
ground cinnamon or grated
   nutmeg to taste

METHOD: Put the bread into a basin, add cold water and leave for 15 minutes then squeeze dry with your fingers. Return the bread to the basin, add all the other ingredients, with enough milk to make a sticky consistency. If the spice is added last you can make quite certain you have the right amount. Put into a greased Yorkshire pudding tin and bake in the centre of a slow oven for $1\frac{1}{2}$ hours or steam in a greased basin for 2 hours.

SUMMER PUDDING

Preparation time: 30 minutes   *Quantity:* 4 helpings

1 lb rhubarb
2 oz prunes (soaked
   overnight)

$\frac{1}{2}$ pint water
8 oz bread
2 oz sugar

METHOD: Stew rhubarb and prunes in the $\frac{1}{2}$ pint of water in which the prunes soaked. Grease a cake tin or pudding basin and line the bottom and sides with fingers of bread, keep odd pieces for putting on top. Strain the juice from the fruit pulp. Soak the bread in the basin thoroughly with the juice. Fill the basin with alternate layers of fruit, sugar, and the trimmings of bread, packing it very tightly and finishing with a layer of bread. Pour over any remaining juice. Place a saucer and weight on top and leave overnight. Turn out and serve with custard.

PADDED PUDDING

Make 1 pint custard sauce, using milk or milk and water but very little sugar; leave in the saucepan. Add 1 teacup fine stale bread-crumbs, 2 tablespoons jam and a few drops vanilla essence to the custard and continue cooking for 5 minutes. Spoon into 4 dishes, allow to cool and top with grated chocolate and Mock Cream as page 61.

FRUIT SHORTCAKE

Cooking time: 15 minutes   *Quantity:* 4 helpings

PASTRY
8 oz self-raising flour with 2
  teaspoons baking powder
  or plain flour with 4
  teaspoons baking powder
pinch salt
1 oz cooking fat

1 dessertspoon sugar
water to mix
FILLING AND TOPPING
½ pint thick fruit purée
Mock Cream 1 or 2 as left
whole fruit

The Ministry of
Food wants your
cooking secrets

METHOD: Sift the flour and baking powder and salt together.
Rub in the fat in the usual way, add the sugar. Mix to a rolling
consistency with cold water. Roll out the pastry into two 7 in
diameter rounds. Put on 2 lightly greased baking trays and bake
near the top of a very hot oven for 15 minutes. Cool then sandwich
with the fruit purée and a little Mock Cream. Top with the whole
fruit and remaining cream. Serve when fresh.

EGG CUSTARDS

You will find that dried eggs can
be used in all your favourite custard recipes in place of fresh
eggs. Reconstitute the egg or
eggs carefully, blend with the
other ingredients and cook in the
usual way.

FRUIT FOAM

Cooking time: 10–15 minutes
Ingredients: 1 lb fruit, prepared
for cooking, little sugar to taste,
Marshmallow Foam, as this page.
Quantity: 4 helpings

Cook the fruit with the sugar and
as little water as possible. Allow
to cool, then beat until a smooth
pulp. Make the Marshmallow
Foam. Allow the fruit to become
quite cold then blend it with the
Marshmallow Foam and spoon
into glasses.

MARSHMALLOW FOAM

Preparation time: 15 minutes   *Quantity:* 4 helpings

1 level teaspoon powdered
  gelatine
¼ pint water

1 tablespoon sugar
3 tablespoons powdered milk
few drops of flavouring

METHOD: Soften the gelatine with about 2 tablespoons of cold
water. Heat the remainder of the water, pour over the gelatine
and stir until dissolved. Add the sugar and gradually whisk in the
milk powder. Continue whisking until the mixture is light and
fluffy. Add the flavouring.

FRUIT SEMOLINA

Cooking time: 20–25 minutes   *Quantity:* 4–6 helpings

1 lb fruit – apples, plums,
  rhubarb or mixed fruit
½ pint water

2 oz sugar
3 oz semolina

METHOD: Cook the fruit to a thick pulp, adding the water and
sugar. It is not essential, but it will give a smoother sweet if it is
then rubbed through a sieve. If not, beat until as smooth as
possible. Bring the pulp again to the boil, whisk in the semolina
and cook gently, stirring from time to time for a good 10 minutes.

VANILLA MOUSE

Put 2 fresh eggs or reconstituted dried eggs into a basin with 1 oz sugar. Whisk over hot water until thick and fluffy. Remove from the water and continue whisking until cold. Make the Marshmallow Foam as opposite page, flavour it with vanilla essense. Gently blend the egg mixture into the Marshmallow Foam. Serves 4–6.

DUTCH FLUMMERY

Cooking time: Few minutes   *Quantity:* 4 helpings

½ pint lemon squash
¾ pint water
½ oz powdered gelatine

2 reconstituted dried eggs or
   fresh eggs
2 oz sugar

METHOD: Put the squash and ½ pint of water into a saucepan and heat. Soften the gelatine with 2 tablespoons of water. Heat the remaining water and pour on to the gelatine. Add the eggs and sugar to the lemon mixture and cook slowly for 5 minutes. Remove the pan from the heat, add the dissolved gelatine, pour into a wet mould and allow to set.

★   ★   ★

MOCK CREAM (1)

Preparation time: 5 minutes   *Quantity:* 2–4 helpings

1 oz margarine
1 oz sugar

1 tablespoon dried milk
   powder
1 tablespoon milk

METHOD: Cream the margarine and sugar. Beat in the milk powder and liquid milk.

MOCK CREAM (2)

Cooking time: 5 minutes   *Quantity:* 2–4 helpings

1 tablespoon cornflour,
   custard powder or
   arrowroot

¼ pint milk
1 oz margarine
1 oz sugar

METHOD: Blend the cornflour or custard powder or arrowroot with the milk, tip into a saucepan and stir over a low heat until thickened, allow to cool. Cream the margarine and sugar until soft and light then very gradually beat in ½ teaspoon of the milk mixture. Continue like this until all the ingredients are mixed well. This makes a thick cream.
For a thin pouring cream use 1 teaspoon cornflour, custard powder or arrowroot.

RECIPE of the WEEK

A SWEET FOR THE CHILDREN'S PARTY

Peel, core and cut ½ lb apples and simmer until tender in ½ teacup water. Sweeten with about 1 dessertspoon honey and flavour with cinnamon or ginger, whichever is liked. Whip the mixture until it is light and frothy. Add half a packet of tablet jelly – strawberry or raspberry is prettiest – and stir well, until it is thoroughly melted. When cool turn into a wet mould. Miniature meringues or ratafia biscuits make a simple decoration for this sweet.

SPECIAL FROM BOURNVILLE

The recipes here form part of a special leaflet produced by Cadburys of Bournville on behalf of the Red Cross. It was sold for 1d. More of the delicious recipes are to be found on page 85.

CHOCOLATE QUEEN PUDDING

Recipe from 'The Kitchen Front'

Cooking time: $\frac{3}{4}$–1 hour
Ingredients: 1 level teacup breadcrumbs, a small knob margarine, 1 level tablespoon sugar, $\frac{1}{2}$ pint milk, 2 level teaspoons, Bournville Cocoa, 4 tablespoons jam or jelly, 2 dried eggs, reconstituted, 1 teaspoon vanilla essence.
Quantity: 4 helpings

Put the breadcrumbs, margarine and sugar in a basin. Boil the milk, cocoa and half the jam and pour it over the breadcrumbs, stirring the mixure well together. Cover with a plate and leave half an hour. Beat eggs thoroughly. Spread a tablespoonful of jam over the bottom of a greased pie-dish. Add eggs and vanilla essence to the breadcrumb mixture. Pour the pudding into the pie-dish and bake about half to three quarters of an hour, in a moderately hot oven till set. Then spread the remaining jam over the top.

CHOCOLATE SPONGE PUDDING

1 oz margarine
2 oz sugar
1 level tablespoon dried egg, dry
8 oz grated raw potato

6 oz flour
1 oz Bournville Cocoa
1 teaspoon baking powder
a pinch of salt
4 tablespoons milk

METHOD Cream fat and sugar together. Mix the dried egg with the raw potato and beat it into the fat and sugar. Mix flour, cocoa, baking powder and salt together and add to the creamed mixture, then stir in enough milk to make a soft dough. Put into a greased pudding basin and steam 1 hour or bake in a pie-dish in the oven 30 to 40 minutes.

FRUIT CHOCOLATE CREAM

apple pulp or fruit in season
2 level tablespoons sugar or more to taste
1 level tablespoon Bournville Cocoa

1 heaped tablespoon flour
$\frac{1}{2}$ pint milk
Mock Cream, page 61

Put the fruit in the bottom of a glass dish or individual glasses. Mix sugar, cocoa and flour to a smooth paste with a little of the milk. Put the remainder on to boil and when boiling pour on to the blended cocoa and flour stirring well. Return to the saucepan, bring to the boil and cook about 8 minutes stirring continuously. Pour over the fruit and when cold top with mock cream. It is advisable to make the chocolate cream in a double pan or in a basin standing in a pan of boiling water.

CHOCOLATE SAUCE

1 oz margarine
1 oz flour
$\frac{1}{2}$ pint milk

$1\frac{1}{2}$ oz sugar
$1\frac{1}{2}$ oz Bournville Cocoa
vanilla essence

Melt margarine in pan. Mix in flour, add milk gradually, then add sugar and cocoa which has been previously blended with a little milk. Bring to the boil stirring all the time. Allow to simmer 5 minutes. Flavour with vanilla and beat well.

FOOD FACTS

preparing for Christmas

Christmas begins in the kitchen and it isn't too soon to begin planning the best use of the Christmas rations now. So here are advance recipes for Christmas fare, all of them tested by practical cooks in the Ministry of Food kitchens.

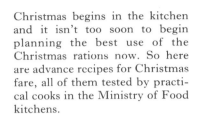

A GOOD DARK CHRISTMAS PUDDING

Cooking time: 4 hours then 2–3 hours   *Quantity:* 6 helpings

2 oz plain flour
½ teaspoon baking powder
¼ teaspoon salt
½ teaspoon grated nutmeg
¼ teaspoon ground cinnamon
1 teaspoon mixed spice
3 oz sugar
½–1 lb mixed dried fruit

4 oz breadcrumbs
2–4 oz grated suet or melted fat
1 oz marmalade
2 eggs or 2 reconstituted dried eggs
¼ pint brandy, rum, ale, stout or milk

METHOD: Sift the flour, baking powder, salt and spices together. Add the sugar, fruit and breadcrumbs and suet or fat. Mix with the marmalade, eggs and brandy, rum or other liquid. Mix very thoroughly. Put in a greased 2 pint basin, cover with greased paper and steam for 4 hours. Remove the paper and cover with a fresh piece and a clean cloth. Store in a cool place. Steam for 2–3 hours before serving.
Note: If the smaller quantities of suet or fat and fruit are used, the pudding should not be made more than 10 days before it is to be used. With the larger quantities you can make it a month before it is to be used.

CHRISTMAS PUDDING WITHOUT EGGS

Mix together 1 cup of flour, 1 cup of breadcrumbs, 1 cup of sugar, half a cup of suet, 1 cup of mixed dried fruit, and, if you like, 1 teaspoon of mixed sweet spice. Then add 1 cup of grated potato, 1 cup of grated raw carrot and finally 1 level teaspoon of bicarbonate of soda dissolved in 2 tablespoons hot milk. Mix all together (no further moisture is necessary) turn into a well-greased pudding basin. Boil or steam for 4 hours.

APPLE MINCEMEAT

Make mincemeat go further by blending it with grated or finely diced raw apples or with thick apple pulp.
If you have not been able to make, or obtain, mincemeat then flavour grated apple with plenty of spices and add a little mixed dried fruit or chopped cooked prunes or chopped raw dates. You then have a pleasant filling for the traditional Christmas tarts.

Snacks & Supper Dishes

The sustaining snacks in this section were suitable for all meals of the day as well as supper time. There are ideas for lunch boxes too, as many people took packed meals with them to work. We were encouraged to eat a cooked breakfast, with everyone working so hard for the war effort they needed a good meal to start the day.

HARD-TIME OMELETTE

Cooking time: 10–12 minutes   *Quantity:* 4 helpings

1½ oz cooking fat
4 medium potatoes, cooked
   and sliced or diced
2 small bacon rashers,
   chopped

3 eggs or reconstituted dried
   eggs
1½ tablespoons water
salt and pepper

METHOD: Heat the fat in a large frying pan or omelette pan. Fry the potatoes and bacon together until crisp and golden in colour. Beat the eggs with the water and seasoning. Pour over the potatoes and bacon and cook until set then fold and serve at once, or serve flat.

POTATO CUTLETS FOR BREAKFAST

These make an excellent start to the day; and one of the beauties of them is that you can prepare them the day before. Scrub 1½ lb potatoes and boil in their skins. When cooked, peel and mash them thoroughly. Scrape ½ lb carrots, boil till tender and mash. Mix the potatoes and carrots together, season with salt and pepper, then shape into cutlets. Dip in browned breadcrumbs, made by baking stale bread in the oven and crushing it. Next morning, place the cutlets in a greased tin and bake in a moderate oven for about 15 mins, or fry them in a very little hot fat.

IRISH OMELETTE

Cooking time: 15 minutes   *Quantity:* 4 helpings

1 lb cooked potato
1 tablespoon chopped parsley
3 oz bacon, chopped
salt and pepper

4 eggs (4 level tablespoons
   dried egg mixed with 8
   tablespoons water)
¼ pint milk or household milk

METHOD: Slice the potatoes and mix with parsley, chopped bacon and seasoning. Put the mixture into a well-greased, pie-dish. Blend the eggs and milk, pour over the other ingredients and bake in a hot oven for 15 minutes.

The Radio Doctor Says:

Health rule for April. It's a good idea to cook potatoes in their jackets. The skin stops the precious Vitamin C from escaping and getting lost in the cooking water. Steaming potatoes is best of all. And never cook them twice.

CRISP CRUST OMELETTE

Cooking time: 5–6 minutes   *Quantity:* 2–4 helpings

2 slices bread
1–1½ oz cooking fat
4 eggs or reconstituted dried
   eggs

2 tablespoons water
salt and pepper

METHOD: Cut the bread into small dice; heat the fat in the frying pan or omelette pan. Fry the bread until crisp and brown. Beat the eggs with the water and seasoning. Pour over the bread, cook until set then fold and serve.

SPANISH OMELETTE

Cooking time: 10 minutes   *Quantity:* 2 helpings

2 eggs (2 level tablespoons
  dried egg mixed with 4
  tablespoons water)
1½ oz margarine or dripping
3 spring onions, chopped

8 oz shredded mixed
  vegetables
2 tablespoons water
a pinch salt and pepper

METHOD: Beat the eggs. Heat the fat in a frying pan and fry the
spring onion and vegetables until tender. Add the eggs, water,
and seasoning, stir until the eggs are set, form into a roll, and
serve immediately.

SAVOURY SCONES

Cooking time: 10 minutes   *Quantity:* 8–10 helpings

4 oz national flour
4 oz medium oatmeal
1 teaspoon baking powder
½ teaspoon salt

2 oz shredded cheese
1 oz fat
household milk or milk and
  water

METHOD: Mix dry ingredients and cheese, rub in fat and work
enough milk or milk and water to make a really soft dough.
Flatten out on floured board, cut in triangles, place on a
greased sheet and bake in a hot oven till brown.

POTATO SCONES

Cooking time: 20 minutes   *Quantity:* 8 scones

4 tablespoons self-raising
  flour
1 teaspoon baking powder
½ teaspoon salt

1 tablespoon margarine or
  cooking fat
4 tablespoons mashed potatoes
milk or household milk

METHOD: Mix together the flour, baking powder and salt, rub in
the fat. Add the potato mashed until light and creamy. Mix all
together with enough milk to make a soft dough. Roll out, form
into rounds and cut into sections with a sharp knife. Brush the
tops with milk, bake in a moderate oven for 20 minutes.

BRIGHT BREAKFASTS SIMPLE—BUT DIFFERENT

Potato Floddies are quick to prepare and are especially appetising
if cooked in the fat left over from
bacon. Grate raw potatoes into a
basin, Mix in enough flour to
make a thick batter, season to
taste, drop spoonsful of the mixture into a pan of hot fat. Fry on
both sides.

Another novelty is slices of
cooked carrot fried with bacon.
Their cheery colour reminds you
of 'bacon and tomatoes', but their
flavour is new and delicious.

What about a cereal? Stale
bread cut in cubes and baked,
makes a crunchy, nourishing
breakfast cereal. Use the heat left
in the oven when you finish the
main cooking.

Rules for Using Dried Egg

1 Store in a cool, dry place and
replace the lid of the tin after use.

2 To turn a dried egg into a
fresh one, mix one level tablespoon of the powder with two
tablespoons of water. This mixture equals one fresh egg.

3 Now treat the egg as you
would a fresh one. Don't make
up more egg than is necessary for
the dish you are making. Beat as
usual before adding to other
ingredients.

SAUSAGEMEAT LOAF

Cooking time: 40 minutes   *Quantity:* 4–6 helpings

12 oz sausagemeat
4 oz corned beef, flaked
1 cooking apple, peeled and grated
1 teaspoon chopped sage or ½ teaspoon dried sage

1 onion, grated
1 tablespoon chutney, chopped finely
2 tablespoons crisp breadcrumbs

METHOD: Mix all the ingredients, except the breadcrumbs, together. Grease a loaf tin or pie dish, coat the bottom and sides with the crumbs. Put in the sausagemeat mixture and bake in the centre of a moderately hot oven for 40 minutes. Serve cold with salad or slice for a packed meal or serve hot with vegetables.

"FADGE" FOR BREAKFAST

"Fadge" is both nourishing and filling for breakfast.

Boil some well-scrubbed potatoes, then peel and mash them while hot. When the mixture is cool enough to handle, add salt, and work in enough flour to make a pliable dough. Knead lightly on a well floured board for about 5 minutes, then roll into a large circle about ¼ inch thick. Cut into wedge shaped pieces and cook on a hot gridle, an electric hot-plate or on the upper shelf of a quick oven until brown on both sides, turning once.

FISH PASTE

3 oz cooked fresh-salted cod
2 oz mashed potatoes
1 oz softened margarine

2 teaspoons Worcestershire sauce
pepper

METHOD: Flake the fish finely with a fork or put through the mincer and beat into the potato until the mixture is smooth and creamy. Then beat in the margarine and sauce and a little pepper. Use for sandwiches.

SEMOLINA SOUFFLÉ

Cooking time: 45 minutes   *Quantity:* 4 helpings

¾ pint milk or milk and water
4 oz semolina
1 small onion, grated
salt and pepper
1 dessertspoon chopped parsley

2 oz cheese, grated
2 eggs or reconstituted dried eggs
2 or 3 tomatoes, sliced

METHOD: Bring the milk or milk and water to the boil; whisk in the semolina, add the onion and seasoning and cook steadily for 10 minutes over a low heat, stirring frequently. Add the parsley, cheese and eggs. Put the tomatoes at the bottom of a greased soufflé or pie dish. Top with the semolina mixture and bake for 30 minutes in the centre of a moderately hot oven. Serve as soon as cooked.

Packed-Meal Menus

Preparing packed meals is quite a job, now that so many of the sandwiches have vanished. But your family still expect something tasty in the dinner packet, and there's no need to disappoint them. Keep a corner of the larder for new and interesting sandwich finds and fillings and try some of the suggestions on these pages.

TO HARDBOIL DRIED EGGS

Reconstitute the eggs; measuring the powder very carefully, see page 67, season lightly then pour into small greased basins or cups. Stand in a pan with a little boiling water and cook gently until set.

MOCK CRAB

Cooking time: 4 minutes   *Quantity:* 2 helpings

½ oz margarine
2 eggs or 2 reconstituted
   dried eggs
1 oz cheese, grated

1 dessertspoon salad dressing
few drops vinegar
salt and pepper

METHOD: Melt the margarine in a saucepan, add the well beaten eggs. Scramble until half set then add the other ingredients. Serve as a sandwich filling or on hot toast or over mashed potatoes.

SAUCY WAYS

A good sauce makes the simplest food more interesting. Try serving cooked vegetables with a white, cheese or parsley sauce. Use some of the vegetable stock in the sauce to save milk and give additional flavour. The Dutch sauce on page 72 is excellent with fish or it can be adapted to make a salad dressing.

WHITE SAUCE

Use margarine or cooking fat for this or dripping.

METHOD: Heat 1 oz fat in a pan, stir in 1 oz flour, cook over a low heat then blend in ½ pint liquid (this can be all milk, milk and water, stock or all vegetable stock). Stir as the sauce comes to the boil and cook until thickened. Season to taste.
Cheese Sauce: Add 1–2 oz grated cheese to the thickened sauce.
Parsley Sauce: Add 1 to 2 tablespoons chopped parsley to the thickened sauce.

RECIPE of the WEEK

SAVOURY SPLITS

These are delicious, filling things to have during a day's hard work or night watch.

Sift 6 oz plain flour with 2 level teaspoons baking powder and ½ teaspoon salt. Mix thoroughly with 4 oz sieved cooked potato (sieved, if possible, when still hot). Rub in 1 oz fat and blend to a soft dough with 4 tablespoons milk. Roll out to ½ in thickness on a well-floured board and cut into rounds. Glaze the tops with a little milk. Bake in a hot oven for 15 minutes. When cold, split the scones and fill with one of these mixtures.
1 Finely diced cooked vegetables bound with a little white sauce.
2 Finely diced cooked beetroots bound with horseradish or some other sharp sauce.
3 Mixed vegetable curry.
4 Shredded raw cabbage heart well mixed with mayonnaise and chopped parsley.

SWEET SPLITS

If you like something in the sweet line, make your splits as above, but for the filling mix some cocoa and sugar (or honey) to a cream with milk. Then work into it a little creamed margarine.

QUICK WELSH RAREBIT

Cooking time: 5 minutes   *Quantity:* 2 helpings

2 slices bread
1 teaspoon margarine
1 teaspoon chutney, or yeast extract

2 tablespoons grated cheese

METHOD: Toast the bread and spread with margarine and a thin coating of chutney, or yeast extract. Cover with grated cheese. Place under the grill till golden brown. Eat with a raw vegetable salad.

POTATO RAREBIT

Used mashed potatoes as a basis for a rarebit. Beat the potatoes until soft and smooth; add a little milk if too stiff. The potatoes should be like a thick cream. Put in as much grated cheese as you can spare with seasoning to taste. Spread on hot toast and brown under the grill.

GOOD EATING

How about these suggestions for new fillings?
1 Shredded cheese and chutney or cooked beetroot.
2 Cooked mashed potato, yeast extract and chopped parsley.
3 Chopped grilled bacon and lettuce.
4 Mashed sardines, pilchards, herring or haddock, mixed with shredded fresh carrot.
5 Minced crisply cooked bacon rinds and toasted oatmeal.
6 Fish paste and chopped parsley.
7 Brawn, shredded swede and chutney.
8 Vegetable or meat extract and mustard and cress.
9 Chopped cold meat and mashed cooked vegetables with seasoning.
10 American sausage meat and watercress.
You may think that some of these ideas will surprise the family, but they'll like them.

OATMEAL CHEESE RAREBIT

Cooking time: 12 minutes   *Quantity:* 4–6 helpings

2 oz flour
$\frac{1}{2}$ pint water
2 oz toasted oatmeal or rolled oats*
2–3 oz grated cheese

1–2 teaspoons salt
$\frac{1}{4}$ teaspoon pepper
little made mustard
4–6 slices toast

METHOD: Blend the flour with a little of the water to make a smooth paste. Bring the remainder of the water to the boil and pour on to the blended flour, stirring well. Return to the pan and, stirring all the time, bring to the boil. Cook gently for 5 minutes then add the oatmeal, cheese and seasoning. Mix thoroughly and divide the mixture equally between the slices of toast. Brown under the grill.

* Spread the oats on to a flat tray and toast in a slow oven

FARMHOUSE SCRAMBLE (1)

Cooking time: 10 minutes   *Quantity:* 2–3 helpings

$\frac{1}{2}$ oz margarine
8 oz mixed raw vegetables, finely grated

2 eggs or reconstituted dried eggs
salt and pepper

METHOD: Melt the margarine in a small pan; add the vegetables and heat until lightly cooked. Beat the eggs with a little seasoning and pour over the vegetables. Scramble lightly and serve with potatoes, as a sandwich filling or on hot toast.

Sandwich making is much easier if you dip the knife in boiling water before spreading the margarine.

Bread mustn't get mouldy now, so keep your bread bin in a dry, airy place. Wipe the bin out every day with a clean, dry cloth, and wash with soda and water once a week. Let new bread cool before putting it in the bin.

Plan your points and obey the rules
Just as you did with your football pools:
You'll find yourself an up-and-upper
At breakfast, dinner, tea and supper!

CHEESE PANCAKES

Cooking time: 15 minutes   *Quantity:* 4 helpings

4 oz flour
1 teaspoon baking powder
2 eggs (2 level tablespoons dried egg mixed with 4 tablespoons water)

½ pint milk
4 oz grated cheese
salt to taste
fat for frying

METHOD: Blend the flour, baking powder and mixed eggs smoothly, add sufficient milk to make a thick, smooth batter. Beat for 10 minutes. Add rest of milk, the grated cheese and salt. Heat a little fat in the frying pan till smoking hot, pour in a thin layer of batter, fry until golden brown on both sides. Turn out, roll, serve with a sprinkling of shredded cheese. Continue until all the batter is used.

CHEESE SAVOURY

Cooking time: 20 minutes   *Quantity:* 4 helpings

1 egg (1 level tablespoon dried egg mixed with a tablespoon water)
½ pint household milk

1 teacup breadcrumbs
4 oz grated cheese
pepper and salt to taste

METHOD: Beat egg with milk. Add the other ingredients. Pour into a greased dish and bake for 20 minutes in a moderate oven until set and brown.

FARMHOUSE SCRAMBLE (2)

Cooking time: 15–20 minutes   *Quantity:* 4 helpings

2 lb mixed cooked vegetables
4 oz grated cheese
3 oz breadcrumbs
chopped parsley

2 eggs (2 level tablespoons dried egg, 4 tablespoons water)
pepper and salt

METHOD: Mix all the ingredients together. Melt a little dripping in a frying pan. When it is hot put in the mixture and spread it over the pan. Put on a saucepan lid and cook for about 20 minutes, shaking occasionally until it is brown. Turn out on a hot dish and serve it with lettuce or shredded cabbage. This dish is just as successful when baked in an oven, but add a little more liquid.

What is the "Oslo Meal"?

What is the "Oslo Meal"? This was a meal originally given as an experiment to school children, and its results in the health and development of the children were remarkable. It makes a satisfying main meal for the whole family —and its simplicity is a great point in its favour with busy housewives. It is salad, bread-and-butter, a glass of milk, *and a piece of cheese.*

LOBSCOUSE

A quickly made dish, very popular with sailors. You'll like it, too! Melt a nut of margarine in a small saucepan, then add 3 oz grated cheese and about 2 tablespoonfuls milk. Stir over a low heat until the cheese is melting, then add two or three tinned or bottled tomatoes, cut in pieces and continue to cook gently until all ingredients are blended. Season with pepper and salt. Serve on a bed of piping hot mashed potato.

The Radio Doctor Says:

'If I were allowed to say only three things on the Kitchen Front, I should say eat some raw green vegetables every day, I should praise milk and more milk and I should preach the virtues of the food which contains so much nutriment—cheese.'

SALAD DRESSING FOR IMMEDIATE USE

Blend 1 level tablespoon household milk powder with 1 level tablespoon dried egg powder, $\frac{1}{2}$ teaspoon salt, a little pepper and dry mustard powder. Add just 1 tablespoon water and 2 tablespoons vinegar and mix until smooth then beat well. Note: It is important that no less than the above amount of vinegar should be used.

DUTCH SAUCE

Cooking time: 10 minutes   *Quantity:* 1 pint

3 oz flour
1 pint milk or household milk or fish stock
3 teaspoons dry mustard
salt and pepper

1 egg (1 level tablespoon dried egg and 2 tablespoons water)
3 to 4 tablespoons vinegar

METHOD: Blend the flour with a little of the milk or fish stock. When smooth add the rest of the liquid and bring to the boil. Cook for 2 to 3 minutes, stirring all the time. Mix the mustard, salt and pepper with the egg and add to the sauce. Stir over a gentle heat, but do not let sauce boil again. Add the vinegar. Stir well and serve (the egg in this recipe is optional). You can use this sauce as Mayonnaise if fish stock is not used.

EGG CHAMP

Cooking time: 20 minutes   *Quantity:* 4 helpings

1 lb potatoes
1 breakfastcup runner beans or any green vegetable
salt and pepper
$\frac{1}{4}$ pint milk

1 oz margarine
4 eggs (4 level tablespoons dried egg mixed with a tablespoon water)

METHOD: Scrub and scrape the potatoes and place in a small quantity of boiling salted water. Cook for 10 minutes and then add the sliced beans. When tender, drain, dry and mash the potatoes with sufficient milk to make smooth and creamy. Add the beans, season well, pile scrambled egg on top of the potato mixture and serve at once. To make the scrambled egg heat 4 tablespoonfuls of milk and the margarine in a pan, add the egg mixture, season and cook over a gentle heat until thickened.

"'Household' milk? Why, ma, that's easy:
(Made this way it can't go cheesy.)
First the water, *then* the powder."
(Mothers never *quite* felt prouder!)

SUPPER SAVOURIES

1 Potato Pasties are always a popular supper. Make a paste by mixing 4 oz mashed potatoes, 2 oz flour and 1 oz dripping with a little cold water. Roll out the paste fairly thin and cut it into rounds. Fill with a mixture of cold cooked vegetables, such as carrots, parsnips and beet. If you have a little cooked meat, so much the better. Mince it and add it to the vegetables seasoned to taste. Damp the edges of the pastry with cold water, fold over and seal. Cut a small hole in the top to let out the steam. Bake in a hot oven for 20 to 30 minutes. These are delicious eaten hot with vegetables and gravy, or, cold, they can take the place of sandwiches.

2 Curried Potatoes make another favourite supper dish. Parboil 2 lb potatoes, and peel them into slices ½ in thick. Make a mixture of 1 dessertspoon curry powder, 1 dessertspoon medium oatmeal and a little salt. Toss the potatoes in the mixture, then arrange in a greased fireproof dish or baking tin, dot with 1 oz dripping and bake in a moderate oven until browned (about 30 minutes).

SORRY! There's no Kraft Cheese or Velveeta now being made!

CHEESE DUMPLINGS

Cooking time: 45 minutes *Quantity:* 4 helpings

1½ lb potatoes, peeled
salt and pepper

2 reconstituted dried eggs
3 oz cheese, grated

METHOD: Cook the potatoes in boiling, salted water, drain and mash; do not add any liquid. Place over a low heat and season well. Add the eggs and 2 oz of the grated cheese. Shape into 8 or 10 round balls and roll in the remaining cheese. Place on a greased baking tin and bake for about 20 minutes in a hot oven until brown and crusty.

CHEESE PUDDING

Cooking time: 30 minutes *Quantity:* 4 helpings

½ pint milk or household milk
2 eggs (2 level tablespoons
  dried egg mixed with 4
  tablespoons water)

4 oz grated cheese
1 breakfastcup breadcrumbs
salt and pepper
¼ teaspoon dry mustard

METHOD: Add the milk to the egg mixture and stir in the other ingredients. Pour into a greased dish and bake for about 30 minutes in a moderately hot oven till brown and set.

CHEESE SALAD

Cooking time: 10 minutes *Quantity:* 4 helpings

1 medium sized cabbage
1½ oz flour
½ pint milk

salt
½ lb cheese, grated
nasturtium flowers

METHOD: Shred the cabbage finely. Blend the flour with a little cold milk, put the remainder on the boil. When boiling pour on to the blended flour, stirring well till smooth. Return to the pan and cook from 1 to 2 minutes. Add salt and grated cheese. Stir until cheese melts. Cool sauce, pour over the finely shredded cabbage, and serve decorated with nasturtium flowers.

"Man-about-Kitchen"

Now that thousands of wives and mothers are helping in the factories, or evacuated to the country, many men are having to do their own cooking. No wonder they ask their women-folk for easy recipes! Here are a few suggestions.

PALETTE SALAD

Preparation time: 10 minutes   *Quantity:* 4 helpings

3 oz cabbage, shredded
4 oz cooked or raw beetroot, grated
2 oz raw parsnip, grated

1 oz raw leek, chopped
2 oz raw carrot, cut in thin strips

METHOD: Lay the shredded cabbage in an oblong dish. Arrange a border of beetroot around the edge of the dish with the other vegetables in strips.

'And if you don't mind prolonging the war, I know just where you can get . . .'

SPRING ON THE KITCHEN FRONT

Spring cleaning takes it out of you—and the only way to put it back is to see that you choose energy-making foods. Here is a meal that won't take much more time to get ready than a cup of tea but which will give you real staying-power.

All you need is one good-size *potato, seasoning, small nut of dripping, a thick frying-pan.*

Chop up the raw potato, melt the dripping in the frying-pan and then spread the potato all over the pan. Press it down firmly into the fat and season well. Then cover with a lid or plate and leave to cook very gently for about ¼ hour. So long as the pan is thick and the heat low, you can then leave it to cook itself. When you dish it up, the under-side of potato will be a golden brown.

MOCK DUCK

Cooking time: 45 minutes   *Quantity:* 4 helpings

1 lb sausagemeat
8 oz cooking apples, peeled and grated

8 oz onions, grated
1 teaspoon chopped sage or ½ teaspoon dried sage

METHOD: Spread half the sausagemeat into a flat layer in a well greased baking tin or shallow casserole. Top with the apples, onions and sage. Add the rest of the sausagemeat and shape this top layer to look as much like a duck as possible. Cover with well greased paper and bake in the centre of a moderately hot oven.

CHEESE SAUCE

Cooking time: 10 minutes   *Quantity:* 2 helpings

1 tablespoon flour
a little dry mustard
1 teacup milk

pepper
1 teaspoon salt
2 oz grated cheese

METHOD: Blend flour and mustard with a little milk and when smooth add the rest of the milk, bring to the boil, cook for 2 to 3 minutes, stirring all the time. Add seasoning and grated cheese, stir over a gentle heat until the cheese is melted.

WHIT SALAD

Preparation time: 15 minutes   *Quantity:* 4 helpings

POTATO EGGS:
½ lb shredded carrot
2 oz grated cheese
¾ lb cooked mashed potatoes
SALAD:
¾ lb cooked, diced potato
1 small shredded cabbage or
    ½ lb spinach
½ lb shredded root vegetables
1 bunch watercress

DRESSING:
½ teaspoon salt
pinch of pepper
1 teacup milk
1 tablespoon vinegar
¼ teaspoon mustard
1 teaspoon sugar
1 teaspoon parsley and 1
    teaspoon mint, chopped
    together

METHOD: To make potato eggs, mix the carrots and grated cheese together and form into balls with a little potato if necessary. Cover the balls with a thick layer of potato and cut in halves. Arrange round the dish to look like hard-boiled eggs. Place the cooked diced potato in the centre of the dish. Add the chopped cabbage or spinach and shredded root vegetables. Decorate with watercress. Make the dressing by mixing all its ingredients together. Serve with the salad.

The Radio Doctor Says:

'As for salad veg I don't mean a lettuce which looks as if it had loved and lost. Lettuce, in fact, is poor in Vitamin C. Go out for the cabbage leaves, the mustard and the cress, and all things raw and beautiful. Ring the changes with endive, chicory, and finely grated carrot, raw beetroot and young dandelion leaves.'

Dig for your dinner

When salvage is all that remains
of the joint
And there isn't a tin and you
haven't a 'point'
Instead of creating a dance and a
ballad
Just raid the allotment and dig up
a salad!

CARROT SANDWICHES FOR A CHANGE

1 Add two parts of grated raw carrot to one part of finely shredded white heart of cabbage, and bind with chutney or sweet pickle. Pepper and salt to taste.
2 Equal amounts of grated raw carrot, cabbage heart and crisp celery bound with chutney or sweet pickle. Pepper and salt to taste.
3 Bind some grated raw carrot with mustard sauce, flavoured with a dash of vinegar.
4 Cook diced carrot in curry sauce until tender enough to spread easily with a knife.

All these fillings taste their best with wholemeal bread.

MOCK GOOSE

Cooking time: 1 hour   *Quantity:* 4 helpings

1½ lb potatoes
2 large cooking apples
4 oz cheese
½ teaspoon dried sage

salt and pepper
¾ pint vegetable stock
1 tablespoon flour

METHOD: Scrub and slice potatoes thinly, slice apples, grate cheese. Grease a fireproof dish, place a layer of potatoes in it, cover with apple and a little sage, season lightly and sprinkle with cheese, repeat layers leaving potatoes and cheese to cover. Pour in ½ pint of the stock, cook in a moderate oven for ¾ of an hour. Blend flour with remainder of stock, pour into dish and cook for another ¼ of an hour. Serve as a main dish with a green vegetable.

Cakes & Baking

We could all manage without cakes, biscuits and scones but these helped to make meals more enjoyable. But the Ministry of Food used to remind us that it was important that all the family ate protective foods first before they enjoyed these home-made treats.

EGGLESS SPONGE

Cooking time: 20 minutes   *Quantity:* 1 cake

6 oz self-raising flour with 1 *level* teaspoon baking powder or plain flour with 3 level teaspoons baking powder
2½ oz margarine

2 oz sugar
1 *level* tablespoon golden syrup
¼ pint milk or milk and water
jam for filling

METHOD: Sift the flour and baking powder. Cream the margarine, sugar and golden syrup until soft and light, add a little flour then a little liquid. Continue like this until a smooth mixture. Grease and flour two 7 inch sandwich tins and divide the mixture between the tins. Bake for approximately 20 minutes or until firm to the touch just above the centre of a moderately hot oven. Turn out and sandwich with jam.

Variation

Eggless Queen Cakes: Use the same recipe but only 6 tablespoons milk or milk and water. Spoon the mixture into about 12 large or 18 small greased patty tins and bake for 10–12 minutes in a hot oven.

COOKING HINTS FOR NATIONAL FLOUR

National flour can be used just as well as white flour in cakes, puddings, pastry, for thickening soups and stews, *but* remember the following points:—

1 Use a little more liquid for mixing, i.e. mix to a softer consistency.
2 Bake, boil or steam a little longer.
3 Add a little more seasoning to savoury dishes.
4 Add more salt and water when making bread.
5 Use a little extra flour for thickening sauces.
6 Use a little less sugar for sweet dishes.

EGGLESS FRUIT CAKE

Cooking time: 1¼ hours **Ingredients:** 10 oz self-raising flour or plain flour with 3 teaspoons baking powder, 1 teaspoon mixed spice, pinch salt, 1 *level* teaspoon bicarbonate of soda, ½ pint well-strained weak tea, 3 oz margarine or cooking fat, 3 oz sugar, 3 oz dried fruit. **Quantity:** 1 cake

Grease and flour a 7 inch cake tin. Sift the flour or flour and baking powder, spice, salt and bicarbonate of soda together. Pour the tea into a saucepan, add the margarine or cooking fat, sugar and dried fruit. Heat until the fat and sugar melt, then boil for 2–3 minutes. Allow to cool slightly, pour on to the flour mixture, beat well and spoon into the tin. Bake in the centre of a moderate oven for 1¼ hours.

★   ★   ★

ONE-EGG SPONGE

Cooking time: 15 minutes   *Quantity:* 1 cake

4 oz self-raising flour or plain flour with 2 teaspoons baking powder
1 oz margarine
2 oz sugar
1 tablespoon warmed golden syrup

1 egg or 1 reconstituted dried egg
½ *level* teaspoon bicarbonate of soda
4 tablespoons milk
little jam

METHOD: Grease and flour two 6 inch sandwich tins. Sift the flour or flour and baking powder. Cream together the margarine, sugar and golden syrup. Beat in the egg, then add the flour. Blend the bicarbonate of soda with the milk, beat into the creamed mixture. Spoon into the tins and bake above the centre of a moderate to moderately hot oven for approximately 15 minutes. Turn out of the tins, cool and sandwich together with a little jam.

SYRUP LOAF

Cooking time: 30 minutes   *Quantity:* 1 loaf

4 oz self-raising flour or plain
   flour with 2 teaspoons
   baking powder
½ teaspoon bicarbonate of
   soda

pinch salt
2 tablespoons warmed golden
   syrup
¼ pint milk or milk and water

METHOD: Sift flour or flour and baking powder, bicarbonate of soda and salt. Heat the syrup and milk or milk and water, pour over the flour and beat well. Pour into a well greased 1 lb loaf tin and bake in the centre of a moderately hot to hot oven for 30 minutes or until firm.

DRIPPING CAKE

Cooking time: 1 hour   *Quantity:* 1 cake

8 oz self-raising flour or plain
   flour with 4 teaspoons
   baking powder
pinch salt
1 teaspoon mixed spice
2–3 oz clarified dripping

2–3 oz sugar
3 oz mixed dried fruit
1 egg or 1 reconstituted dried
   egg
milk or milk and water to
   mix

METHOD: Sift the flour or flour and baking powder, salt and mixed spice. Rub in the dripping, if this is very firm grate it first. Add the sugar, fruit, egg and enough milk or milk and water to make a sticky consistency. Put into a greased and floured, 7 inch cake tin. Bake in a moderate oven about 1 hour.

SPICE CAKE

Cooking time: 1½ hours
Ingredients: 4 oz dried fruit, 3 oz margarine or lard, 2 oz sugar, 1 teaspoon mixed spice, dusting of grated nutmeg, 1 teacup water, 8 oz self-raising flour or plain flour with 4 teaspoons baking powder, 2 oz golden syrup, 1 tablespoon milk, 1½ teaspoons bicarbonate of soda. **Quantity:** 1 cake

Put the fruit, margarine or lard, sugar, spices and water into a good-sized saucepan, bring to the boil. Simmer for 5 minutes and leave until quite cold. Turn into a bowl and fold in the flour or flour and baking powder. Warm the syrup with the tablespoon of milk in the saucepan, stir in the bicarbonate of soda, immediately blend with the rest of the ingredients. See that the soda is thoroughly mixed in or the cake will be streaky instead of richly brown all over. Turn into a greased cake tin and bake in a slow oven for 1½ hours.

Saving Paper *Always save butter and margarine paper; they are just the thing for lining cake tins*

VINEGAR CAKE

Cooking time: 1 hour   *Quantity:* 1 cake

6 oz self-raising flour
3 oz margarine
3 oz sugar
¼ pint milk

1 tablespoon vinegar
½ teaspoon bicarbonate of
   soda
3–4 oz mixed dried fruit

METHOD: Sift the flour. Cream the margarine and sugar. Pour the milk into a large basin, add the vinegar and bicarbonate of soda; the mixture will rise and froth in the basin. Blend the flour and vinegar liquid into the creamed margarine and sugar then add the dried fruit. Put into a greased and floured 7 inch tin, bake in a moderate oven for 1 hour.

DARK STICKY GINGERBREAD

Cooking time: 50 minutes   *Quantity:* 1 cake

6 oz self-raising flour or plain
    flour with 3 teaspoons
    baking powder
pinch salt
1 teaspoon bicarbonate of
    soda
1 teaspoon ground ginger
1 teaspoon ground cinnamon
    or mixed spice

1 tablespoon dried egg, dry
2 oz cooking fat or dripping
    or margarine or peanut
    butter
2 oz sugar
2 good tablespoons black
    treacle or golden syrup
$1\frac{1}{2}$ tablespoons milk
6 tablespoons water

METHOD: Line a tin about 7 by 4 inches with greased greaseproof paper or use margarine or cooking fat paper. Sift the dry ingredients into a mixing bowl. Put the fat (or alternatives), sugar, treacle or syrup into a saucepan, heat until melted, pour on to the dry ingredients, add the milk and beat well. Put the water into a saucepan in which the ingredients were melted and heat to boiling point, stir well to make sure no ingredients are wasted then pour on to the other ingredients and mix. Pour into the tin and bake in the centre of a very moderate oven for 50 minutes or until *just* firm. Cool in the tin for 30 minutes then turn out.

Variations

If you want a dark gingerbread and have no black treacle, add 1 teaspoon gravy browning to the other ingredients.
Moist Orange Cake: Follow the recipe above; omit the spices and use marmalade instead of treacle or golden syrup.

Prices of
DRIED FRUITS

From tomorrow dried fruits will be classified into 3 groups with a maximum price for each group, so that you will be able to buy what there is at really reasonable prices throughout the United Kingdom.

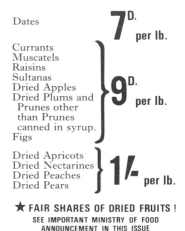

Dates	**7**D. per lb.

Currants
Muscatels
Raisins
Sultanas
Dried Apples
Dried Plums and
  Prunes other
  than Prunes
  canned in syrup.
Figs
	9D. per lb.

Dried Apricots Dried Nectarines Dried Peaches Dried Pears	**1/-** per lb.

★ FAIR SHARES OF DRIED FRUITS !
SEE IMPORTANT MINISTRY OF FOOD
ANNOUNCEMENT IN THIS ISSUE

WATER BISCUITS

These are like the biscuits we used to buy before the war to serve with cheese.

Sift 8 oz plain flour and $\frac{1}{2}$ teaspoon salt. Rub in 1 oz cooking fat and mix with water to make a firm dough. Knead well and roll out until paper thin. Cut into rounds or squares, put on to ungreased baking sheets and bake for 3–4 minutes towards the top of a very hot oven. The biscuits blister if they are rolled sufficiently thin.

WELSH CAKES

Cooking time: 8–10 minutes   *Quantity:* Makes about 12

2 oz dripping
6 oz self-raising flour or plain
    flour and 3 teaspoons
    baking powder
$\frac{1}{4}$ teaspoon ground nutmeg
2 oz sugar

2 oz mixed dried fruit
    (including some chopped
    dates or grated carrot)
1 reconstituted dried egg or 1
    fresh egg
1 tablespoon milk

METHOD: Rub the fat into the flour or flour and baking powder and add the spice, sugar and dried fruit. Mix to a stiff dough with the egg and milk. Treat the mixture as pastry and roll out to $\frac{1}{4}$ inch in thickness. Cut into 3 inch rounds. Preheat and grease a griddle or heavy frying pan. Put in the Welsh Cakes and cook for 4 minutes, or until golden brown on both sides.

GINGER PARKIN

Cooking time: 50 minutes   *Quantity:* 1 cake

4 oz self-raising flour with 1 teaspoon baking powder or plain flour with 3 teaspoons baking powder
1 level teaspoon bicarbonate of soda

2 oz margarine or cooking fat
3 oz medium oat meal or rolled oats
1 oz sugar
2 tablespoons golden syrup
5 tablespoons milk

METHOD: Line a tin about 7 by 4 inches with greased greaseproof paper or use margarine or cooking fat paper. Sift the dry ingredients together, rub in the margarine or cooking fat, then add the oatmeal or rolled oats, sugar, golden syrup and milk and beat well. Spoon into the lined tin and bake in the centre of a moderate oven for 50 minutes or until firm.

Variation

Ginger Sponge Parkin: Use 6 oz flour and omit the oatmeal or rolled oats. Reduce the liquid to 4 tablespoons. Bake as above and split the cake and fill with jam and a Mock Cream, page 61.

GINGER AND DATE CAKE

Cooking time: 50 minutes   *Quantity:* 1 cake

7 oz self-raising flour or plain flour with 3 teaspoons baking powder
1 teaspoon bicarbonate of soda
1 teaspoon ground ginger
2 oz cooking fat, dripping or margarine

2 tablespoons golden syrup
1–2 oz sugar
2–3 oz dates, chopped
1 egg or 1 reconstituted dried egg
3 tablespoons milk or milk and water

METHOD: Line a tin about 7 × 4 inches with greased greaseproof paper or use margarine or cooking fat paper. Sift the dry ingredients together. Put the fat, dripping or margarine, syrup and sugar into a saucepan. Heat until melted. Add the dates and allow to stand for a few minutes then blend these ingredients and the egg with the flour mixture. Heat the milk or milk and water in the saucepan in which the fat was melted, stir well to make sure none of the ingredients are wasted. Pour on to the rest of the cake ingredients, beat well. Spoon into the tin and bake in the centre of a very moderate oven for 50 minutes. Cool in the tin for 20 minutes, then turn out.

FLAKED BARLEY CAKE

Cooking time: 45–50 minutes **Ingredients:** 6 oz self-raising flour or plain flour with 3 teaspoons baking powder, ¼ teaspoon salt, 3 oz margarine, 3 oz sugar, 3 oz flaked barley, 4 tablespoons milk or water, 2 tablespoons jam. **Quantity:** 1 cake

Sift together the flour or flour and baking powder and salt. Rub in the margarine, add 2 oz of the sugar and the barley and mix to a stiff dough with the milk or water. Divide the mixture in half and shape into two equal sized rounds, about ½ inch thick. Put one round on a greased baking sheet and cover with jam. Place the other round on top, sprinkle with the rest of the sugar and bake in a hot oven for 20 minutes. Lower the heat to moderate and cook for a further 25–30 minutes until the cake is cooked through.

Reflect, whenever you indulge
It is not beautiful to bulge
A large, untidy corporation
Is far from helpful to the Nation

ROCK BUNS

Cooking time: 10–12 minutes   *Quantity:* 10–12 cakes

8 oz self-raising flour or plain flour with 4 teaspoons baking powder
½ teaspoon mixed spice, if desired
2 oz margarine or cooking fat or dripping
2 oz sugar

2 oz mixed dried fruit, chopped if required
1 egg or 1 reconstituted dried egg
milk or milk and water to mix
2 teaspoons sugar for topping

METHOD: Sift the flour or flour and baking powder and spice. Rub in the margarine, fat or dripping; add the sugar, dried fruit and the egg. Gradually add enough milk or milk and water to make a sticky consistency. Put spoonfuls on to one or two greased baking sheets. Sprinkle with the sugar and bake in a hot to very hot oven for 10–12 minutes.

Variation

Jam Buns: Omit the dried fruit in the Rock Buns. Put the plain mixture on to baking trays. Make a dip in the centre of each cake with a floured finger and put in a little jam. Bake as above.

HONEY OATMEAL BUNS

These nourishing buns are extremely popular in most homes. Try them on your family. This recipe makes 18 medium-sized or 12 larger buns.

Sift 4 oz white flour, 1 heaped teaspoon baking powder and some salt. Then rub in 2½ oz margarine or clarified cooking fat. When evenly mixed, add 4 oz fine oatmeal and a level teaspoon ground ginger. Mix a little beaten-up egg with 3 dessertspoons honey (loosened by slight warming if necessary) and mix to a stiff consistency with a fork. You may need a little milk here. Divide the mixture into roughly piled heaps. Bake in a hot oven for quick rising; then reduce the heat slightly for crisp, even browning. The whole baking should take about 20 minutes.

MAIDS OF HONOUR

Cooking time: 15–20 minutes
Ingredients: shortcrust pastry made with 6 oz flour, etc. see page 53, little jam, 1 oz margarine, 1–2 oz sugar, ½ teaspoon almond essence, 3 oz fine breadcrumbs, 2 tablespoons milk. **Quantity:** 12–15 tarts

Make the pastry, roll out thinly and line 12–15 patty tins, top with a little jam. Cream the margarine, sugar and almond essence, add the breadcrumbs and milk. Spoon the top over the jam and bake in the centre of a moderately hot oven until firm and golden.

The Queen of Hearts
Said 'No' to tarts
'There's Wheatmeal
Bread for Tea.
Each cream-gold slice
Is oh, so nice
And better far for me.'

ROLLED OAT MACAROONS

Cooking time: 15–20 minutes   *Quantity:* 15–16 biscuits

3 oz margarine
2 oz sugar
½–1 teaspoon almond essence
1 tablespoon golden syrup

4 oz self-raising flour
4 oz rolled oats
milk to mix

METHOD: Cream the margarine, sugar, almond essence and syrup. Sift the flour, add to the creamed ingredients with the rolled oats. Mix thoroughly then add just enough milk to make the mixture bind together. Roll into 15–16 balls and put on to greased baking trays, allowing room to spread. Bake for 15–20 minutes or until golden brown in the centre of a moderate oven. Cool on the baking trays then remove.

CARROT COOKIES

Cooking time: 20 minutes   *Quantity:* 12–15 cakes

1 tablespoon margarine
2 tablespoons sugar and a
little extra for sprinkling
on tops of the cakes
a few drops vanilla, almond
or orange flavouring

4 tablespoons grated raw
carrot
6 tablespoons self-raising
flour or plain flour and $\frac{1}{2}$
teaspoon baking powder

WE'VE A LOT TO TELL YOU....

OATMEAL

You will find hints and recipes
for many simple and interesting
ways to use us and other foods
. . . IN THE NEWS
read FOOD FACTS in the
newspapers every week.
. . . ON THE AIR
listen to the Kitchen Front
Talks at 8.15 am weekdays.

(To get a full tablespoon of margarine or fat, plunge the spoon first into boiling water, then cut out the fat with the hot spoon. In this way, a piece of just the right quantity will be obtained.)

METHOD: Cream the fat and sugar together until it is light and fluffy. Beat in the flavouring and carrot. Fold in the flour or flour and baking powder. Drop spoonfuls of the mixture into small greased patty pans. Sprinkle the tops with sugar and bake in a brisk oven for about 20 minutes.

FRUITY POTATO CAKES

Cooking time: 9–10 minutes   *Quantity:* 10–12 cakes

4 oz cooked potatoes
2 oz self-raising flour with $\frac{1}{2}$
teaspoon baking powder or
plain flour with 1 teaspoon
baking powder
1 oz margarine

1 oz sugar
1 tablespoon marmalade
1 oz dried fruit
TOPPING
sugar and mixed spice, if
desired

METHOD: Mash or sieve the potatoes until light and floury; do not add any milk. Sift the flour and baking powder, mix with the potatoes. Cream the margarine, sugar and marmalade, then add the flour and potato mixture with the dried fruit. Mix together. Put on to a floured board and roll out with a floured rolling pin. Cut into 10–12 rounds or triangles.

Grease a heavy frying pan, solid electric hotplate or griddle with a greased paper. Heat for a few minutes then test by shaking on a little flour. The heat is correct when the flour turns golden brown within 1 minute. Put on the potato cakes. Cook for 2 minutes on either side then lower the heat and cook gently for another 5–6 minutes. Serve cold or hot.

The cakes can be sprinkled with a little sugar and mixed spice.

BAKING POWDER DOUGHNUTS

Cooking time: 8–9 minutes **Ingredients:** 8 oz self-raising flour with 2 teaspoons baking powder or plain flour with 5 teaspoons baking powder, pinch salt, 2 tablespoons sugar, 2 tablespoons dried egg, dry, 4 tablespoons water, $\frac{1}{4}$ pint milk, 2 oz fat, sugar for coating. **Quantity:** 8–10 doughnuts

Sift together all the dry ingredients, gradually beat in the water and milk. Heat the fat in a large frying pan, drop in spoonfuls of the mixture. Cook quickly for 2 minutes on either side then lower the heat and cook more slowly for 4–5 minutes. Lift out of the pan, sprinkle with a little sugar. Serve hot or cold.

RAISIN CRISPS

Cooking time: 20 minutes   *Quantity:* 24 biscuits

3 oz self-raising flour or plain
   flour with 1 teaspoon
   baking powder
1 tablespoon dried egg, dry
1 oz sugar

1 oz margarine
1 oz raisins, chopped
few drops almond essence
milk to mix

METHOD: Mix flour, dried egg and sugar together. Rub in the margarine, add the raisins, almond essence and enough milk to make a firm dough. Roll out thinly and cut into rounds (about 2 inches in diameter). Bake in the centre of a moderate oven for 20 minutes.

HOW TO MAKE OATCAKES

Oatmeal, one of the finest foods for giving warmth and energy, is a 'must' for growing children. They will probably like it as Oatcakes, made this way.

Mix together 8 oz fine oatmeal, $1\frac{1}{2}$ oz self-raising flour and $\frac{1}{2}$ teaspoon salt. Add 1 tablespoon dripping, melted, and enough boiling water to bind. Roll out the mixture as thinly as possible in a little fine oatmeal. Cut it into triangles and bake on a greased tin in a fairly hot oven.

OATMEAL BISCUITS

Mix $\frac{1}{4}$ lb flour, $\frac{1}{4}$ lb oatmeal, $\frac{1}{2}$ teaspoonful salt and $\frac{1}{2}$ teaspoon baking powder. Rub in 2 oz margarine, add 1 teaspoon sugar or syrup and mix to a stiff dough with milk or milk and water, half and half. Turn out on to a floured board and roll to about $\frac{1}{2}$ inch thickness. Cut into squares, place on a greased tin and bake in a moderate oven for 15 minutes.

DROP SCONES

These are a favourite recipe in Scotland where they are known as Scotch Pancakes.

Sift 4 oz plain flour with 2 level teaspoons of baking powder and a pinch of salt. Add 1 tablespoon dried egg powder then beat in $\frac{1}{4}$ pint milk and 2 tablespoons water.

  Grease and heat a heavy frying pan, electric solid hotplate or griddle. To test if the right heat, drop on a teaspoon of batter, this should turn golden brown on the bottom in 1 minute. Put the mixture in tablespoons on to the plate and leave until the top surface is covered with bubbles then turn and cook on the second side. The scones are cooked when quite firm.

POTATO DROP SCONES

Rub 2 oz mashed potato into 4 oz flour and $\frac{1}{4}$ teaspoon salt. Make into a stiff batter with half a beaten egg and $\frac{1}{4}$ pint milk. Allow to stand for a time. Sift in a small teaspoon of cream of tartar and a small level teaspoon of bicarbonate of soda and $\frac{1}{2}$ oz sugar just before cooking. Cook in spoonfuls—as for Drop Scones—on a greased girdle or in a heavy frying pan. Serve with a little hot jam.

COFFEE POTATO SCONES

Sift 6 oz plain flour, 2 level teaspoon baking powder and $\frac{1}{2}$ teaspoon salt into a basin. Mix thoroughly with 4 oz mashed potato. Rub in 2 oz fat with the tips of the fingers. Blend to a soft dough with $\frac{1}{2}$ teacup strong, milky, sweetened coffee. Roll out to $\frac{1}{2}$ inch thickness on a floured board and cut into rounds. Glaze the tops with a little milk. Bake on greased baking sheets in a hot oven for 15 minutes.

On this and the next 2 pages are a selection of recipes devised by Cadbury's which formed a leaflet which sold for 1d. in aid of the Red Cross. The rest of the recipes, which were for puddings, are on page 62.

CHOCOLATE SQUARES

Melt 3 oz margarine with two tablespoons of syrup in a saucepan, mix in ½ lb rolled oats and a pinch of salt. Blend well, and put in a greased, shallow baking tin, flattening the mixure smoothly. Bake for half an hour to 40 minutes in a moderate oven. Take out, and whilst still hot, grate over it a tablet of chocolate. The chocolate will melt with the heat, and can be spread evenly with a knife. Cut into squares and lift out.

CHOCOLATE LAYER CAKE

3 oz fat
1 tablespoon syrup or treacle
8 oz flour
½ teaspoon salt
1 good oz Bournville cocoa

1 teaspoon baking powder
½ teaspoon bicarbonate of soda
2 oz sugar
about ½ pint warm water

METHOD: Put fat and syrup into pan and dissolve. Mix all dry ingredients in basin and stir in melted fat and syrup, mix to a very soft consistency with warm water. Pour into two greased sandwich tins and bake about 30 minutes in a moderate oven. Turn cakes out and when cold, sandwich them with Mock Whipped Cream or chocolate spread.

MOCK WHIPPED CREAM

½ oz cornflour
¼ pint milk
1½ oz margarine

3 teaspoons sugar
few drops vanilla essence

METHOD: Mix cornflour to a paste with a little milk, heat remainder and when boiling add to the blended cornflour, stirring well. Return to saucepan bring to boil and cook 3 minutes. Cream the margarine and sugar. Whisk in the cornflour mixture gradually. Add vanilla essence.

CHOCOLATE SPREAD

1 oz Bournville cocoa
1½ tablespoons sugar

1 dessertspoon flour
½ cup milk

METHOD: Mix dry ingredients. Add the milk gradually and bring to the boil. Beat until quite smooth. Allow to cool.

CHOCOLATE CAKE

6 oz flour
2 teaspoons baking powder
1 oz Bournville cocoa
2 oz fat
1 or 2 dried eggs, dry

2 oz sugar
3 saccharin tablets
a little milk and water
few drops vanilla essence

METHOD: Sieve flour, baking powder and cocoa together. Cream fat, egg and sugar. Add dry ingredients alternately with the saccharins dissolved in warm milk and water and essence and mix well. Bake in moderate oven about 50 minutes.

CHOCOLATE BISCUITS

Melt 2 oz margarine and 1 tablespoon warmed syrup. Mix in 1 oz Bournville cocoa, 4 oz flour, 2 oz sugar, $\frac{1}{4}$ teaspoon bicarbonate of soda and 1 teaspoon vanilla essence. Beat well, roll out cut into squares, place on a baking sheet and prick. Bake in a moderate oven about 15 minutes. Sandwiched together with chocolate spread page 85.

TEA-TIME FANCIES

2 oz fat
2 oz sugar
1 level tablespoon Bournville cocoa
1 dried egg, reconstituted

4 oz self-raising flour
1 level teaspoon baking powder
pinch of salt
about 2 tablespoons milk

METHOD: Cream fat and sugar, add cocoa and beat in the egg. Sift together flour, baking powder and salt and stir into the mixture alternately with a little of the milk until the consistency is soft and creamy. Put a spoonful of the mixture into greased and floured patty pans and bake about 20 minutes in a moderate oven. When cold slice off the tops, spread liberally with Mock Cream page 61 and replace tilted to show the filling.

CHOCOLATE FLAVOURING

All the family will enjoy cakes and biscuits given a chocolate flavour, this is easily achieved as you will see from the recipes on the various pages.

GLOSSY CHOCOLATE ICING

METHOD: Mix together 2 teaspoons melted margarine, 1 tablespoon cocoa powder, 1 tablespoon golden syrup and a few drops of vanilla essence.

CHOCOLATE OAT CAKES

1 oz margarine and
1 oz cooking fat
8 oz self-raising flour
1 breakfastcup rolled oats

2 oz sugar
salt
$1\frac{1}{2}$ oz Bournville cocoa
milk and water

METHOD: Rub fats into flour. Add oats, sugar, salt and cocoa. Mix well adding a little milk and water to moisten. Roll out very thinly, cut into rounds and prick all over with a fork. Bake in a moderate oven about 15 minutes till golden brown.

AMERICAN PIN WHEELS

PASTRY
8 oz flour
pinch of salt
$\frac{1}{4}$ teaspoon bicarbonate of
  soda
$\frac{1}{2}$ teaspoon cream of tartar
or 1 teaspoon baking powder
2 oz margarine

milk to mix
CHOCOLATE MIXTURE
2 oz margarine
2 tablespoons sugar
1 dessertspoon Bournville
  cocoa
$\frac{1}{2}$ teaspoon vanilla essence

PASTRY: Put flour, salt, soda and cream of tartar in a bowl. Mix together, rub in margarine and bind to a stiff paste with milk.

CHOCOLATE MIXTURE: Cream margarine and sugar together, stir in cocoa, add essence, and if necessary a tablespoonful of milk; do not make too soft or the mixture will run during cooking. Roll out pastry into an oblong and spread with chocolate mixture. Roll up as for jam roll and cut into $\frac{3}{4}$ inch rounds. Pack into a baking tin and bake in a moderately hot oven 20 to 30 minutes.

CHOCOLATE CAKE

2 oz margarine or cooking fat
2 oz sugar
few drops vanilla essence
1 tablespoon warmed golden
  syrup
5 oz self-raising flour or plain
  flour with 2 teaspoons
  baking powder

$\frac{1}{2}$ teaspoon bicarbonate of
  soda
1 oz Bournville cocoa
2 eggs or 2 reconstituted
  dried eggs
Milk or milk and water to
  mix
jam

METHOD: Cream together the margarine or cooking fat, sugar, vanilla essence and golden syrup. Sift the flour or flour and baking powder, bicarbonate of soda and cocoa. Add the eggs gradually to the creamed ingredients then the cocoa mixture and lastly enough milk or milk and water to make a soft consistency. Divide the mixture between two 7 inch greased and floured sandwich tins. Bake just above the centre of a moderate to moderately hot oven for 20–25 minutes or until firm to the touch. Cool and sandwich together with jam. The cake can be topped with Glossy Chocolate Icing, left.

RECIPE of the WEEK

STEAMED CHOCOLATE CAKE

Cooking time: $1\frac{1}{2}$ hours
Ingredients in a saucepan: 1 breakfastcup milk, 2 tablespoons syrup, 2 oz margarine or lard
Ingredients in a bowl: 1 breakfast cup self-raising flour, $1\frac{1}{2}$ tablespoons sugar, 2 tablespoons Bournville cocoa, 1 teaspoon bicarbonate of soda, 1 dessertspoon vinegar
Quantity: 1 cake
Method: warm ingredients in a saucepan, stirring them together. Meanwhile mix together ingredients in bowl mix very thoroughly. See that there are not any lumps of bicarbonate left. Pour warm sauce out of pan into bowl and stir all together adding vinegar. Pour mixture into a 7 in greased and floured cake tin, cover with greased paper and an inverted saucer. Steam for $1\frac{1}{2}$ hours.
Note: One small gas jet will cook cake and a steamed pudding at the same time, one above the other.

SCOTCH SHORTBREAD

This is an exceptionally economical recipe.

METHOD: Melt 2 oz margarine, add 4 oz plain flour and 1 oz sugar and mix well then knead with your fingers until the mixture binds together. Put on to an ungreased baking tin and press hard to form into a neat round about ½ inch in thickness. Mark into 6–8 sections; prick with a fork and bake in the centre of a moderate oven for 20 minutes.

ICING

(made with sugar and household milk)

4 level dessertspoons sugar	2 tablespoons water
6 level tablespoons household milk, dry	colouring flavouring

METHOD: Mix sugar and milk powder together. Add water and beat till smooth. Add colouring and flavouring and spread on top of cake.

GINGERBREAD MEN

Cooking time: 20 minutes   *Quantity:* 6–8 men

2 oz sugar or golden syrup	few drops lemon substitute
2 oz margarine	1 level teaspoon bicarbonate
8 oz plain flour	of soda
½ level teaspoon mixed spice	1 tablespoon tepid water
2 level teaspoons ground ginger	little reconstituted egg few currants

METHOD: Melt in a pan the sugar or syrup and margarine. Pour into a bowl, add some of the flour, the spices and lemon substitute. Stir well. Dissolve the bicarbonate of soda in the water, add to the mixture, continue stirring, gradually adding more flour. Finish the process by turning out the mixture on to a well-floured board. Knead in the remainder of the flour. Roll a small ball for the head, flatten it and place it on a greased baking tin, roll an oblong for the body and strips for arms and legs. Join these together with a little of the egg and put currants for the eyes. Continue like this until you have made 6–8 'men'. Cook in the centre of a moderate oven for 20 minutes. Cool then remove to a wire tray. Store in an airtight tin.

RECIPE of the WEEK

UNCOOKED CHOCOLATE CAKE

This is a special treat for children who could make it themselves if they are old enough to heat food in a saucepan.

Put 2 oz margarine, 2 oz sugar and 2 tablespoons golden syrup into a saucepan. Heat gently until the margarine has melted and then remove from the heat. Stir in 2 oz cocoa powder and a few drops of vanilla essense then 6 oz crisp breadcrumbs. Mix well. Grease a 7 inch sandwich tin with margarine paper then put in the crumb mixture. Allow to stand for 4 or 5 hours then turn out carefully. Top with Glossy Chocolate Icing, made as the recipe on page 86.

SIMNEL CAKE

Cooking time: 1 hour   *Quantity:* 1 cake

8 oz self-raising flour or plain
   flour with 4 teaspoons
   baking powder
pinch salt
1 teaspoon mixed spice
$\frac{1}{2}$ teaspoon ground nutmeg
$\frac{1}{2}$ teaspoon ground cinnamon
2 oz margarine or cooking fat

$1\frac{1}{2}$ oz sugar
8 oz mixed dried fruit,
   chopped
1 tablespoon golden syrup
1 tablespoon marmalade
$\frac{1}{4}$ pint milk and water to mix
Mock Marzipan to decorate,
   right

METHOD: Sift the flour, baking powder if used, salt and spices together. Rub in the fat and add the sugar and fruit. Mix to a stiff consistency with the syrup, marmalade and milk and water. Turn into a greased 6 or 7 inch tin and bake in a moderate oven for 1 hour. When cold, cut in half, place a layer of Mock Marzipan between the two halves and decorate the top with the remaining paste.

CHOCOLATE COATING FOR YOUR CHRISTMAS CAKE

Mix together 3 tablespoons of sugar with 2 tablespoons of cocoa and 2 tablespoons of milk. Stir, in a stout saucepan, over a low heat until the mixture is thick and bubbly like toffee, then, while hot, pour it over your cake.

A Christmassy sparkle is easy to give to sprigs of holly or evergreen for use on puddings. Dip your greenery in a strong solution of Epsom salts. When dry it will be beautifully frosted.

MOCK MARZIPAN

Ingredients: 2 oz margarine, 2 tablespoons water, 2–3 teaspoons ratafia or almond essence, 4 oz sugar or golden syrup, 4 oz soya flour

Melt margarine in the water, add essence and sugar or syrup then soya flour. Turn on to a board and knead well. Roll out, cut to a circular shape with the tin the cake was baked in. Smear the top of the cake with jam or jelly then cover with marzipan. The cake can be topped with icing as below.

Turn on your wireless at 8.15 every morning and listen to the Kitchen Front for useful tips and recipes.

CHRISTMAS CAKE

Cooking time: 2 hours   *Quantity:* 1 cake

3 oz sugar
4 oz margarine
1 level tablespoon golden
   syrup
8 oz plain flour
2 teaspoons baking powder
pinch salt
1 level teaspoon mixed spice

1 level teaspoon ground
   cinnamon
2–4 reconstituted dried eggs
1 lb mixed dried fruit
$\frac{1}{2}$ teaspoon lemon substitute
   or essence
milk to mix

METHOD: Cream the sugar and margarine, add the syrup. Mix the flour, baking powder, salt and spices together. Add alternately with the eggs to the creamed mixture and beat well. Add the fruit, lemon substitute or essence and enough milk to make a fairly soft dough. Line a 7 inch tin with greased paper, put in the mixture and bake in a very moderate oven for 2 hours.

This cake should keep about 2 months if stored in a clean, dry, airtight tin. Do not store until quite cold. Examine from time to time to make sure it is keeping all right.

Preserving

It is always a source of satisfaction and of pride to have one's own home-made jams, jellies and pickles. But when the Battle of the Atlantic was raging it was up to each one of us to preserve every ounce of home grown fruit and vegetables we could. So we searched our gardens and the fields and hedgerows for all the produce we could find and preserved them for the winter.

Bottling without Sugar

. . . and if you follow these directions, it will be bottling without tears or fears. Home-grown fruits are grand ship savers and every ounce possible must be saved.

OVEN METHOD

1 Wash and drain jars.
2 Pack fruit tightly, almost to top of jar.
3 Place in a very low oven (gas mark $\frac{1}{4}$, 240 F) on cardboard or several thicknesses of paper. Jars should be covered with the lids (without rubber rings) to prevent fruit from burning.
4 Leave in oven for $\frac{3}{4}$ hour to 1 hour (allow $1\frac{1}{4}$–$1\frac{1}{2}$ hours for apricots, pears and peaches) until fruit is cooked. Fruit shrinks in cooking so top up with fruit from one of the jars.
5 Remove jars from oven one at a time, place on wooden table and cover fruit with boiling water.
6 Tap jars to expel bubbles.
7 Seal at once with rubber rings, lids and clips or screw-bands. The screw-bands should be tightened as jars cool.
8 Test next day by removing screw-bands or clips. If seal is perfect you can lift jars by lids. Screw-bands should be dried, lightly greased and put on again loosely. Clips should not be replaced.

TOP-OF-THE-STOVE METHOD

1 Wash and drain jars.
2 Pack jars tightly with fruit until almost full.
3 Cover fruit with cold water, filling jars to overflowing.
4 Fix on rubber rings (already soaked in cold water) and lids by clip or screw-bands. (Give screw-band a half-turn back to allow for expansion.)
5 Take a fish kettle, zinc bath, bucket, or any pan deep enough for water to cover jars. Put a piece of wood or other packing in the bottom. The jars mustn't touch each other or the saucepan. Cover the jars with cold water.
6 Bring the water very slowly to simmering point. (This should take $1\frac{1}{2}$ hours.) Simmer for 15 minutes. (Apricots, Pears and Peaches need 30 minutes.)
7 Remove jars from saucepan. Place on wooden table, tighten screw-bands.
8 Test next day as above.

Even more bottles and rings have been sent out to the shops this year than last—but demand is heavier too. Manufacture is still going on, so if you don't succeed in buying at the first attempt it is worth trying again. You may be able to use old rubber rings, but test them first for elasticity.

HOW TO USE CAMPDEN TABLETS

1 Dissolve Campden Tablets in cold or tepid water, allow 1 tablet to each $\frac{1}{2}$ pint of water.
2 Pack the fruit into jars to within an inch of the top. Do not pack too tightly.
3 Pour over the Campden solution until fruit is entirely covered. (Approximately $\frac{1}{2}$ pint of solution for each pound of fruit.)
4 Seal at once with rubber rings, clips or screw-bands and glass lids.
5 When fruit is required for use it must be boiled first in an open pan to get rid of preservative. This usually takes about 15 minutes.
6 If metal covers are used, protect metal by fitting 2 or 3 layers of paper in lid.

Preparing for Winter!

APPLE RINGS

Here's a way of keeping apples that can be used for windfalls or blemished fruit. Wipe the apples, remove the cores and peel thinly. Cut out any blemishes. Slice into rings about $\frac{1}{4}$ inch thick. Steep the rings for 10 minutes in water containing $1\frac{1}{2}$ oz of salt to the gallon. Thread the rings on sticks or canes to fit across the oven or spread on trays. Dry very slowly until they feel like chamois leather. The temperature should not exceed 150°F. Turn once or twice during cooking.

Pears can be treated in the same way, but they must be cut in halves or quarters and spread on the trays.

PARSLEY HONEY

Cooking time: $\frac{3}{4}$ hour   *Quantity:* 1 lb

5 oz parsley (including stalks)   1 lb sugar
$1\frac{1}{2}$ pints water $\frac{1}{2}$ teaspoon vinegar

METHOD: Pick parsley and wash well. Dry. Chop stalks up roughly. Put into a pan with $1\frac{1}{2}$ pints of boiling water and boil until it reduces to a pint. Strain. Add 1 lb sugar and boil until syrupy (like honey) about 20 minutes, then add $\frac{1}{2}$ teaspoonful of vinegar. Pour into pots and cover. This jells by the next day, and tastes and looks like heather honey.

QUESTIONS YOU ASK

HOW CAN I PRESERVE TOMATOES?

One way is to pulp them. Wash, and cut the tomatoes into quarters; and, if liked, add $\frac{1}{4}$ oz each of salt and sugar to every 2 lb tomatoes. Heat in a covered saucepan until quite soft. Rub the pulp through a sieve, return to the pan and bring to the boil. Have ready clean, hot jars. Fill the jars one at a time with the boiling hot pulp and seal it immediately before proceeding to next jar. Keep the pan on the heat all the time. Seal with four rounds of thin paper cut large enough to come well down the outside of the jars. Brush each round of paper with well-boiled paste and press, one above the other, tightly over the neck of the jar. Tie tightly with string while the paste is still wet.

Another method is to plunge the tomatoes, whole, into boiling water for half a minute, then into cold water. Peel them, put into screw-band or clip-top jars. Cover the tomatoes with brine made with $\frac{1}{2}$ oz salt to 1 quart water; add $\frac{1}{4}$ oz sugar, if liked. Put on the lids and sterilise in the same way as for bottled fruit but raise the temperature to 190°F in $1\frac{1}{2}$ hours and maintain for 30 minutes.

Does Campden Solution Destroy Food Value in Fruits?

No. When required for use, of course, the fruits preserved by this simple method must be boiled to get rid of the preservative, but this lowers the vitamin value only as much as ordinary cooking.

Food for the picking

Blackberrying is a traditional custom that most of us have enjoyed at one time or another. There are other Hedgerow Harvests too, that provide good things for the larder. So why not take the children and go a-harvesting? Be sure, however, that in their excitement they do not damage bushes or hedges, or walk through growing crops, or gather mushrooms in fields without getting the farmer's permission.

GOOD JAMS AND JELLIES

Use the freshest fruit possible and try and pick or buy this when it is just ripe, but not over soft or bruised in any way. Use the amount of sugar recommended in reliable recipes if you want the jam or jelly to keep well. Each jar should contain 60% sugar content for perfect keeping quality, i.e. each 1 lb sugar should produce 1⅔ lbs jam or jelly. Cover the jars well and store in a cool dry place.

Several easy to make and less usual jams, marmalades and preserves are given.

Cooking or crab apples make a lovely jelly, so do other fruits with lots of flavour. There is no need to peel or core apples, simply cut them into pieces (you could use windfalls providing all bruised parts are cut away). To each 2 lb fruit allow 1 pint water. Simmer the fruit slowly to extract all the pectin then put through a jelly bag or several thicknesses of muslin to extract the juice. Measure this and allow 1 lb sugar to each 1 pint juice. Stir the heated juice and sugar until all the sugar has dissolved then boil rapidly until setting point is reached.

For a new flavour try mixing blackberries or rose hips with the apples.

Elderberries are delicious stewed with half-and-half apple; or made into jam with an equal quantity of blackberries. Wash and strip them from the stems.

Sloes look like tiny damsons. They are too sour to use as stewed fruit, but make a delightful preserve with marrow.

Rowan-berries (Mountain Ash) make a preserve with a pleasant tang, admirable to serve with cold meats. You can make the preserve of the berries alone, or with a couple of apples to each pound of berries.

Hips and Haws should not be picked until perfectly ripe. Hips—the berries of the wild rose, make a vitamin-rich syrup. Haws—the berries of the may-tree, make a brown jelly that is very like guava jelly.

Nuts. Cobnuts, walnuts, chestnuts and filberts are good keepers. Choose very sound well-coloured nuts. Remove them from their husks, spread them out and leave to dry overnight. Pack cobnuts and filberts tightly into jars or crocks and cover with an inch layer of crushed block salt. Pack walnuts and chestnuts in a similar manner but cover with sand instead of salt. Packed in this way your nuts should keep till Christmas. Beechnuts make good eating, too. Store them as you would cobnuts. Use as almonds.

Mushrooms are very easy to dry and make an excellent flavouring for winter soups and dishes. Small button mushrooms are best for drying. Gather them in the early morning; simply spread them out to dry in the air for a few days.

ORANGE AND APPLE MARMALADE

Occasionally we are able to bring fresh oranges into the country for young children. Keep the peel and use it to make marmalade.

METHOD: Take the peel from 1 lb sweet oranges (this is 3–4 oranges). Shred this finely. Put into 2½ pints cold water and soak overnight. Simmer the peel in the water until tender and the liquid reduced. Add 1 lb peeled cooking apples (weight when peeled) to the peel and liquid. Simmer until the apples make a smooth purée.

Measure the apple and orange mixture. To each 1 pint pulp allow 1 lb sugar. Put the pulp and sugar back into the pan, stir over a low heat until the sugar has dissolved, then boil rapidly until setting point is reached. Put into hot jars and seal.

ELDERBERRY AND APPLE JAM

Cooking time: about 1 hour   *Quantity:* about 6 lbs

3 lb elderberries   5 lb sugar
3 lb apples

METHOD: Remove berries from stalks and wash. Warm them to draw juice. Simmer for ½ hour to soften skins. Core apples and simmer until quite soft in another pan with very little water, pass through sieve or pulp well with wooden spoon, add apples to elderberries, reheat and add sugar. Stir until dissolved and boil rapidly until jam sets. Make first test for setting after 10 minutes. Put into hot jars and seal.

BLACKBERRY AND APPLE JAM

Cooking time: ¾ hour   *Quantity:* about 5 lbs

Here is a favourite recipe:
1½ lb sour apples   4 lb firm blackberries
1 breakfastcupful water   4½ lb sugar

METHOD: Peel, core and slice the apples. Put in the preserving pan with the water and cook till quite soft. Add the blackberries and bring to the simmer. Simmer for 5 minutes, then add the sugar (warmed) and boil rapidly until setting point is reached. (Make first test after 10 minutes.) Put into hot jars and seal.

Rose-Hip Syrup

This syrup is suitable for infants, very palatable and so rich in Vitamin C that 1 oz is sufficient for 1 month. It is 15–20 times as rich as orange juice.

2 lb rose hips, ripe and red, 1 lb 2 oz sugar

Wash hips and put into a stainless pan. Well cover with water and bring to the boil. Simmer until tender (about 10 minutes). Mash well with a wooden spoon. Put into a jelly bag made of flannel and squeeze out as much juice as possible. Return pulp to the saucepan and add as much water as at first. Bring to the boil and simmer for 5–10 minutes. Put back into jelly bag and squeeze again. Empty bag and wash it thoroughly. Mix the two lots of juice and pour into the clean jelly bag. Allow to drip overnight. A clean juice is now obtained free from the hairs that cover the seeds inside the fruit which might cause irritation if not removed.

Boil the juice down until it measures about 1½ pints, then add 1 lb 2 oz sugar. Stir until dissolved, boil for 5 minutes. Bottle while hot in perfectly clean hot bottles and seal at once. Small screw-capped bottles with rubber washers are suitable. A circle of rubber cut from an old hot water bottle or cycle inner tube, and boiled for 10 minutes to sterilise will do for a washer. The syrup should be stored in a dark cupboard.

A saltspoonful (15 drops) should be sufficient for an infant each day.

They'll be welcome this winter

P EAS AND BEANS are very nourishing and they are easy to preserve and to store. *Drying* is the best method for peas and broad beans; *salting* is the best method for runner and French beans. Think how your family will enjoy these summer vegetables on a winter's day! Here is how to do it:

Salting Beans

Salting is the best way of preserving runner or French beans. Use young fresh beans. Take a lb of cooking salt to 3 lb of beans. Wash the beans, dry, string them and, if large, break into pieces. Crush the salt with a rolling pin. Put a layer of salt about 1 inch deep into the bottom of a crock or jar. Press in a layer of beans, then another layer of salt $\frac{1}{2}$ inch deep, and so on. The secret of success is to pack the salt well down on the beans. Finish with a layer of salt 1 inch deep. Cover with paper and tie down. Leave for few days for beans to shrink. Add more beans and more salt until jar is full again. If beans are well covered with salt it doesn't matter how moist they are. Re-cover. Store in a dry cool place. Before use, wash beans thoroughly in hot water, then soak for 2 hours in warm water. Cook without salt.

DRYING Begin by dropping the peas or broad beans (shelled) into boiling water; boil for two or three minutes, drain. This improves the colour. Next, if you have time, 'pop' the skins off; the peas or beans then fall into halves and dry more quickly. All vegetables should be dried as quickly as possible, but be careful not to scorch them.

IN THE OVEN Spread the vegetables thinly on cake racks or trays made by nailing wooden slats together for frames, and tacking tightly stretched canvas or other open material across the bottoms (old curtain net will do). Put the trays in the oven (temperature not more than 150° Fahrenheit) and leave the door slightly open as this allows the moisture to escape. If you have a dial regulator, take no notice of it, but use the tap to adjust the heat, or you can use the heat left after baking, and so save fuel. In this case give the vegetables a good hour or so, then continue the next day. Several periods of such drying will do no harm.

IN THE AIRING CUP-BOARD Spread the vegetables on muslin, place on the hot water tank or on the hottest shelf in the cupboard and leave for several days with the door ajar.

WHICHEVER METHOD YOU USE, continue drying until the peas or beans are quite crisp. Then leave them for twelve hours to get cold. Store them in paper bags, or pieces of paper tied with string, in tins or jars. Look them over occasionally to see they're all right.

MAKING GOOD PICKLES

Pickles and chutneys help to make meals more interesting so are worth making. Choose good quality vegetables for pickles. It is very important to have pure malt vinegar; this may be a little difficult to find, but it is worth while searching for it.

Cover pickles and chutneys carefully, never put metal tops directly on to the preserve, line the inside of a metal top with thick paper or cardboard; this prevents the top becoming rusty and spoiling the top of the contents of the jars.

★ NOW — before you forget it —

cut out this advertisement, put it up in your kitchen and make a start with your vegetable and fruit preserving. Think what a thrill it will be for your family in the dark days of winter when you serve such treats as summer peas, beans, pears, plums and apples of your own preserving.

PICKLED CUCUMBERS

If the cucumbers are very small they can be left whole, but otherwise cut into convenient sized pieces.

Put into a brine made with 2 oz cooking salt to 1 pint cold water. Soak overnight. Allow 1 level tablespoon mixed pickling spices to each pint of vinegar. Boil vinegar and pickling spices for 15 minutes, strain and cool. Remove the cucumber from the brine, rinse well under the cold tap, then drain thoroughly. Pack into jars, pour over the cold vinegar and seal carefully.

APPLE CHUTNEY

Cooking time: 45 minutes   *Quantity:* $3\frac{1}{2}$ lb

8 oz onions, grated or finely chopped
$\frac{1}{2}$ pint malt vinegar
2 lb apples, weight when peeled and chopped
1 teaspoon pickling spices
1 teaspoon salt
1 teaspoon ground ginger
12 oz sugar
2–4 oz dried fruit (if desired)

METHOD: Put the onions into a saucepan with a little vinegar and simmer until nearly soft. Add the apples, spices tied up securely in a muslin bag, salt, ground ginger and just enough vinegar to stop the mixture from burning. Cook gently until the fruit is soft, stirring from time to time. Add the remainder of the vinegar and thoroughly stir in the sugar and dried fruit. Boil steadily until the chutney is thick. Remove the bag of pickling spices and pour the hot chutney into hot jars. Seal down at once.

MUSTARD PICKLES

Cooking time: 15–20 minutes   *Quantity:* $2\frac{1}{2}$ lb

2 lb mixed vegetables
brine—see under Pickled Cucumber
1 pint vinegar
1 tablespoon pickling spice
2 oz sugar
1 tablespoon flour or $\frac{1}{2}$ tablespoon cornflour
1 dessertspoon ground ginger
$\frac{1}{2}$ tablespoon tumeric powder

METHOD: Cut the vegetables into neat pieces. Soak overnight in brine. For quantities of brine, see Pickled Cucumbers, this page. Wash well under the cold tap and drain thoroughly. Boil the vinegar and pickling spice together. Mix all the dry ingredients with a very little vinegar until a smooth paste, pour over the strained hot vinegar and stir well. Return to the pan and cook until just thickened. Put in the vegetables and cook for 5 minutes. Put into jars and seal well.

PICKLED ONIONS AND SHALLOTS

Remove outer skins from the onions or shallots, using a stainless knife to prevent their discolouring.

Soak in brine for 48 hours. For quantities see Pickled Cucumbers. Then proceed as for that recipe.

Making Do

It was a challenge to all of us to 'make do' in every way, to save fuel and use our food wisely. We may not have been able to produce exactly the same dishes as we did before the war, but we could still keep our families well fed. The government gave us many ideas and dealt with various problems and many other people passed on their tips.

5 DISHES FROM 1 RECIPE

Ingredients: 1 level tablespoon dried egg (dry)*, 4 oz flour, pinch of salt, ½ pint of milk and water mixed. **Method:** Mix dry ingredients. Add sufficient liquid to make a stiff mixture. Beat well, add rest of liquid and beat again. *Dried eggs are new-laid shell eggs with shell and water removed.

YORKSHIRE PUDDING

Make a knob of fat smoking hot in a tin and pour in the batter. Cook in brisk oven for 30 minutes.

TOAD-IN-THE-HOLE

Use batter with sausages or meat left-overs. Cook for 30 minutes.

SWEET PANCAKES

Make a knob of fat 'smoking' hot in frying pan. Cook each pancake separately (this makes 6 pancakes), browning on each side. Add jam while in pan; roll up.

SAVOURY PANCAKES

Same as above, using fried onions or leeks, grated cheese or chopped cooked vegetables.

BATTER PUDDING

Same as Yorkshire Pudding; omit salt, add sugar and fruit (dried apples or bottled plums). Cook and serve in baking dish.

New ways with Carrots

'I can see why they tell us to eat a lot of home grown carrots', says Mrs. Harass 'but what else can you do with them except boil them?'

Carrots have many uses, not only in soups and stews but to sweeten puddings (they even take the place of apricots, as in the recipe on page 52) and in Cookies (page 83). They are delicious baked round a joint or in Carrot Jam (recipe opposite or in this Marmalade.

CARROT AND SEVILLE ORANGE MARMALADE

This recipe has been tested by the Research Station at Long Ashton. It yields about 5½ lb of marmalade.

Wash 1¼ lb Seville oranges and squeeze out the juice. Collect all the pips into a muslin bag. Cut up the peel fairly coarsely and place it, with the juice and bag of pips, in a basin. Cover with 2 pints of water and leave overnight. Next morning, simmer gently until the peel is quite tender and the weight of pulp is 2½ lb. Remove the pips.

Cook 2 lb carrots (weighed after scraping) in a pint of water, in a covered saucepan until tender, and then mash well or rub through a wire sieve.

Add the carrot pulp and the water to the orange, bring to the boil, add 2 lb sugar and boil rapidly until of a fairly thick consistency (25 to 30 minutes).

As this marmalade contains little sugar it will not keep longer than a week or so, unless hermetically sealed. This may be done either by using fruit bottling jars or making an airtight seal to the jam jars with a synthetic skin which is now on the market. In either case the covered jars should be immersed while hot in a pan of hot water brought to the boil, and boiled for 5 minutes. The marmalade will then keep for months.

Every night our stout-hearted lorry drivers are risking their lives to bring you food. They don't let you down— so don't let them down by wasting food.

Wholesome is as wholesome does...

CARROT JAM

When fruit is unobtainable and you have sugar for jam you can use carrots or swedes to eke out the fruit.

METHOD: Cook 8 oz peeled carrots in a little water until a smooth pulp. Cook 1 lb sliced cooking apples (weight when peeled) in ¼ pint water until a smooth pulp. Mix the carrot and apple pulps together. Measure this and to each 1 pint allow 1 lb sugar. Tip back into the saucepan, stir until the sugar has dissolved, then boil until stiffened. This never becomes as firm as a real fruit jam.

HONEYCOMB TOFFEE

Cooking time: 8 minutes   *Quantity:* 6 oz

4 oz golden syrup
2 oz sugar (Demerara if possible)

2 level teaspoons bicarbonate of soda

METHOD: Boil the syrup and sugar together for about 5 minutes or until it is a rich brown colour. While still boiling stir in the bicarbonate of soda very quickly. Pour into a well-greased sandwich tin and allow to cool and set. When almost firm, loosen edges with a knife and turn out on to a wire tray. Break into pieces.

SOME
Delicious Drinks

Anyone can make them who has a garden or can easily get to the countryside.

MINT TEA

Cover the bottom of a large jug with freshly gathered sprigs of mint. Pour on some freshly made weak tea or plain boiling water. Strain and serve. Make with dried mint in the winter using a little more than fresh mint. Strain well.

BLACKBERRY LEAF TEA

Pick tender green leaves when dry if possible. Cut them up with a stainless knife. Spread them out and dry thoroughly in the shade or in an airy room; this may take four days or longer. Don't pick or dry them in the sun. Store in an airtight tin and turn them out fairly frequently to air and prevent going mouldy. Make just like ordinary tea. Or, if you like your tea strong, cook for five minutes after making. Serve without milk, add a little sugar if liked. Delicious and very like Indian tea.

BARLEY WATER

Wash 2 oz barley, put into a pan with 2 pints of cold water. Simmer for 2 hours. Strain, add a little sugar and the juice from some sharp fruit such as rhubarb or redcurrants or lemon flavouring.

WOOLTON PIE

Cooking time: about 1 hour   *Quantity:* 4 helpings

This pie is named after the Minister of Food—Lord Woolton. It is an adaptable recipe that you can change according to the ingredients you have available.

Dice and cook about 1 lb of each of the following in salted water: potatoes (you could use parsnips if topping the pie with mashed potatoes), cauliflower, swedes, carrots—you could add turnips too. Strain but keep ¾ pint of the vegetable water.
    Arrange the vegetables in a large pie dish or casserole. Add a little vegetable extract and about 1 oz rolled oats or oatmeal to the vegetable liquid. Cook until thickened and pour over the vegetables; add 3–4 chopped spring onions.
    Top with Potato Pastry or with mashed potatoes and a very little grated cheese and heat in the centre of a moderately hot oven until golden brown. Serve with brown gravy.
    This is at its best with tender young vegetables.

**Listen to the
Kitchen Front
at 8.15
every morning**

*To-day's Scraps
To-morrow's Savouries*

You must make the best of every ounce of food you have. Even odds and ends left over from your meals mustn't be thrown away. Here are some suggestions for using-up:
1 Chop up odd scraps of cold meat and bake in a batter.
2 Left-over beans make splendid fillings for pastry turnovers.
3 Use up cooked fish in a salad or as a sandwich filling.

QUESTIONS YOU ASK

'What can I give baby instead of orange juice?'
The juice squeezed from raw blackcurrants. Baby will need only half as much blackcurrant juice as orange. The Government is making arrangements this season for canning and bottling blackcurrant juice, so that it will be available next winter.

'Can you give me a suggestion for a nourishing meatless meal?'
Have a variant of the 'health meal' lately tried for school children, with excellent results to their health. Instead of meat and vegetables, they had wheatmeal bread and butter and salad, as much as they could eat, with cheese and a glass of milk. Instead of the cheese when you have used their ration give herring, or, when you can get pulses, cold lentil rissoles or pease pudding.

WELSH MUTTON

Cooking time: 2 hours   *Quantity:* 4 helpings

For a meal for four people, get 1½ lb of scrag end of mutton. That costs 6d and is less than half one person's weekly ration. The other ingredients are:

4 large leeks	1 pint of water
3 carrots	salt to taste
6 potatoes	

METHOD: Cut up the mutton and put it in a saucepan with tepid salted water. Bring it to the boil. Take off the brown scum and simmer for an hour. Cut the leeks into 3-inch lengths, and add, with the cut-up carrots, to the pan, and simmer for half an hour. Then add the potatoes, peeled and quartered. Simmer for another 20–30 minutes.

VICTORIA SANDWICH

Cooking time: 25 minutes   *Quantity:* 1 cake

2 oz of margarine
2 oz of sugar
2 dried eggs, used dry
5 oz of plain flour

2 tablespoons water
4 level teaspoons of baking
  powder

METHOD: Cream the fat and sugar and beat in the dried eggs. Mix the flour and baking powder and add them a little at a time to the creamed margarine and sugar, alternating with the water. Add a little milk if necessary but the mixture ought to be fairly stiff. Put into two greased tins and bake in a fairly hot oven. Turn out onto a wire rack. Sandwich together with one of the following fillings.

Amusing little figures cut from short-crust or biscuit dough, go down well. Roll the dough about ¼-inch thick. 'People' can be made by cutting small rounds for heads, larger for bodies, strips for arms and legs; pinch the various pieces of dough firmly together. Mark eyes, noses, mouths, with currants. If you can draw a little or have a friend who can, make thin cardboard 'patterns' of animals, lay them on the dough and cut round with a small sharp knife.

WHITE ICING

Cooking time: 5 minutes **Ingredients:** 2 fluid oz water, 2 oz sugar, 2 oz milk powder. **Quantity:** Sufficient for 1 cake

Boil water and sugar together. Allow to go off the boil, then add the milk powder and mix well together. Use to cover 1 medium sized cake.

VARIATIONS IN CAKE FILLINGS

Cooking time: 5 minutes   *Quantity:* to fill 1 cake

Here is the basic recipe for a cake filling which will not be either solid or runny, just thick enough to stay where it is meant to:

2 level tablespoons of dried
  egg
2 level tablespoons of flour
1 level tablespoon of sugar

5 level tablespoons of
  Household milk powder
1 pint of water

METHOD: Mix the dry things, including the milk powder dry (see that there are no lumps) and then blend to a smooth cream with some of the water. Bring the rest of the water to the boil and pour slowly on to the blended mixture; then put the whole lot back in the pan and boil, still stirring, for a couple of minutes. Beat it a bit as it gets cold and you will find you will have something you can reasonably call a cream.

Like that it won't taste very exciting, but there are hundreds of ways you can vary it and here are a few. You can make it taste of chocolate by adding 4 level tablespoons of cocoa before blending. The bottled flavours can be added at the end: then you can be sure of getting the taste you want. A few drops of vanilla is wonderful in chocolate cream, but hardly enough perhaps on its own. Lemon is good, or lemon and orange mixed. Or any of the fruit flavourings you like; or peppermint. Try making some chocolate and some peppermint and using them together; or putting peppermint filling inside a chocolate cake. But whatever kind you make, taste it when it is cooked and then sweeten to taste.

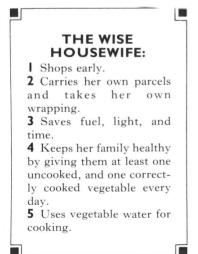

THE WISE HOUSEWIFE:

1 Shops early.
2 Carries her own parcels and takes her own wrapping.
3 Saves fuel, light, and time.
4 Keeps her family healthy by giving them at least one uncooked, and one correctly cooked vegetable every day.
5 Uses vegetable water for cooking.

After the War

It was wonderful when the strain of the war was over, but a fact many people do not appreciate was that food rationing continued for many years after the end of hostilities. Certainly some foods gradually became more plentiful and new foods, such as whale meat appeared. The advice from the Ministry of Food was still appreciated and so were the many broadcasts about food and recipes.

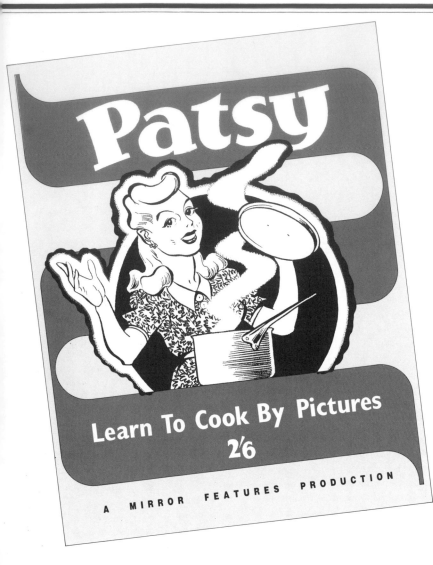

SAVE THAT FAT

Many people know the trick of skimming the fat off the top of their stews when cold. But how many people know how to make best use of their fat?

Collect all the oddments of fat you can from frying pans, baking tins and stews. Melt and strain them all into a big bowl and wash them by pouring on some boiling water (you will need about a pint of water for 2 oz fat). When the liquid solidifies, lift off the solid fat and scrape the sediment off the bottom; it is now quite suitable for frying or roasting. Wise housewives will take this a step further. They will heat the fat up again until it stops bubbling. This means that it is quite free from moisture and will keep literally indefinitely. It can be used for anything, even cake making.

PUMPKIN SOUP

Cooking time: about 45 minutes   *Quantity:* 4 helpings

1 onion
2 lbs pumpkin
water to cover
1 oz margarine

salt and pepper
milk as required
1 egg

METHOD: Chop up the onion. Peel the pumpkin, remove the seeds and slice. Place in a pan together with the onion and enough water to cover and cook until tender, then strain. Return to the heat, adding the margarine and salt and pepper to taste. Then add enough milk to make a nice creamy consistency and bring to a boil. When you feel it has cooked through enough, take off the heat and add a well-beaten egg. Serve.

PEA PURÉE PANCAKES

Cooking time: 25 minutes   *Quantity:* 4 helpings

1 lb peas (fresh, dried or tinned)
½ teaspoon sugar
dab of margarine

1 dessertspoon chopped mint
salt and pepper
pancakes or fried croûtons
2 oz grated cheese

METHOD: Cook the peas until tender. Add a little sugar to the water as this brings out the flavour of the peas. Drain and mash the peas and then mix in the margarine, mint and seasoning. When you've made the pancakes spread the purée between two as though for a sandwich and serve with grated cheese. Alternatively you could serve the purée very hot in bowls like a soup adding croûtons. The croûtons are made by cutting bread into cubes and frying in very hot fat.

SEVEN WAYS TO STUFF POTATOES

Cooking time: about 1¼ hours
Ingredients: 1 large potato per person, 2 tablespoons grated cheese per person, dab of margarine, a little milk, pepper and salt, filling. **Quantity:** 1 helping

Bake the potatoes in their jackets. When they are cooked cut a hole in the middle (a little bigger than a half crown) and scoop out the inside. Put the potato into a heated bowl with the cheese, margarine, milk and seasoning. Mash together. Then put back into the potato making a hollow so that it can be filled by any one of these: 1) scrambled eggs, 2) left-over mince, 3) left-over curry, 4) beans in tomato sauce, 5) left-over fish with some added flavouring, 6) sausage meat mixed with onion and sage, 7) scrambled egg mixed with some bacon. The potatoes are then returned to the oven to heat through. A lovely hot meal for winter.

RECIPE of the WEEK

MOCK OYSTER PUDDING

Cooking Time: 30 minutes
Ingredients: 5 medium soft roes, 2 oz dried breadcrumbs, ½ pint milk, 1 oz melted margarine, 2 dried eggs reconstituted, 1 teaspoon sugar, salt and pepper, a little nutmeg.
Quantity: 4 helpings

Rinse the roes, and drain well. Chop finely. Mix with the breadcrumbs, milk, margarine, eggs, sugar, seasoning and nutmeg. Turn into a greased piedish. Bake till golden brown in a moderately hot oven about 30 minutes.

BAKED HERRING SANDWICH

Cooking time: 30 minutes   *Quantity:* 1 helping

herring
seasoning

margarine
2 slices bread

METHOD: Remove the scales, head and tail of the herring. Open it flat and clean out removing the bones. Then sprinkle lightly with salt and pepper. Spread the margarine on the bread (make a good coating) and then put the herring between the slices and bake in a hot oven until well browned. This should be served very hot and is ideal as a breakfast or supper dish.

MUTTON MOULD

Preparation time: 10 minutes   *Quantity:* 4 helpings

2 cups cooked mutton
1 slice stale bread
2 cups any cooked vegetables
chopped parsley, lemon,
  thyme

chives or small onion,
  chopped
seasoning
dash Worcester sauce
½ pint thick white sauce

METHOD: Mince the mutton, bread and vegetables and then mix well. To this add the chopped herbs, onion, seasoning and Worcester sauce (or any other sauce). Stir in the white sauce making sure you keep the mixture as thick as possible. Spoon into a wet mould. It is ready to eat when cold and can be served with a salad or as a delicious sandwich filler. This recipe is a good way of using up those odds and ends as well as dealing with sometimes tough meat.

DEVON MILK

Preparation time: 30 minutes   *Quantity:* 4 helpings

¾ pint of thick sour milk
1 level tablespoon raspberry
  jam or stewed raspberries

1 dessertspoon sugar
a white of egg

METHOD: Strain the sour milk in a muslin so that the whey is drained and only the thick curd is left. Transfer this into a bowl and add the sugar and raspberry jam (or stewed raspberries). Lightly beat the egg white and then whisk this together with the rest of the ingredients and serve chilled in a glass dish.

RABBIT SURPRISE

Cooking time: 1½ hours   *Quantity:* 4 helpings

small rabbit
1½ pints of water
1 teaspoon of salt
½ pint of rice
fat for frying

1 onion or 3 spring onions
3 tomatoes
½ teaspoon of pepper
pinch of ginger or cayenne
½ pint brown gravy

METHOD: Bone the rabbit and cut into bite sized pieces. Boil up some salted water and pour in the rice and leave to cook for about 15 minutes. While you're waiting for it to cook you can be preparing the rabbit. Heat up the fat and gently cook the pieces of rabbit until a golden brown. Drain the cooked rice and to it add thinly chopped onion(s), sliced tomatoes, pepper and ginger or cayenne. Place a little of this mixture onto a greased casserole dish and then lay the rabbit on top. With the remainder of the rice mixture cover the rabbit add half a pint of gravy. Cover the casserole and cook gently for about an hour.

APPLE BUTTER

This spread makes a substitute for butter. After cutting out any damaged parts of the apples, wash and quarter them, but don't peel or core. Then place in a pan with enough water to cover and cook slowly until soft. After straining off juice rub the apples through a sieve. For every pound of pulp use ½ lb sugar. Add the sugar to the juice and bring to a boil, add pulp and continue to cook until the mixture is thick and smooth, remembering to stir to prevent catching. Pot into small jars and seal while hot. (Once opened it is better to use up quickly) Flavouring can also be added. For example the equivalent of an orange or lemon to 1 lb of pulp or even vanilla to taste; also quarter teaspoon of cinnamon or a few cloves could be added.

RECIPE FOR CHOCOLATE

Cooking time: about 5 minutes   *Quantity:* ¾ lb

1 tin household milk
2 tablespoons cocoa or grated chocolate
2 oz sultanas

4 oz margarine
1 cup sugar
2 tablespoons milk (or may need a little more)

METHOD: Mix household milk, cocoa or chocolate and sultanas together. Heat margarine, sugar and milk in saucepan, pour into household milk mixture and mix well. Pour into a greased sandwich tin and leave to cool. Cut into pieces. It is ready to eat, but even better next day.

GYPSY CREAMS

Cooking time: 10 to 15 minutes   *Quantity:* about 20

2 cups rolled oats
1 cup plain flour
½ cup sugar
1 teaspoon bicarbonate of soda

2 oz margarine
2 oz lard
1 tablespoon syrup
1 tablespoon water

METHOD: Mix the dry ingredients; melt the fat, syrup and water, without boiling, and add to the dry ingredients to form a stiff consistency. Make into small balls about the size of hazelnuts. Flatten slightly, and bake in a moderate oven for 10–15 minutes. When golden brown, cool on a wire tray. Sandwich together with a filling of butter icing, flavoured according to taste with chocolate, orange or vanilla. A little dried milk and syrup helps to stretch this filling.

HONEY CAKES

Cooking time: about ¼ hour **Ingredients:** 1 level teaspoon sugar, 2½ margarine, 2 level tablespoons honey, 6 oz self-raising flour, 1 level teaspoon cinnamon. **Quantity:** 16 to 20

Beat together the sugar and margarine until the mixture is soft and creamy, then add the honey. Sift together the flour and cinnamon. Add to the creamy mixture with a spoon until it binds together then work it with your fingers until it is a soft smooth dough. Flour your hands, take off a piece of dough about the size of a large walnut and roll between the palms of hands until it is a smooth ball. Put on to a slightly greased tin and flatten slightly. Continue until all the dough has been used up. Bake in a moderately hot oven until the cakes are done—about 15 minutes.

Index